THE BUUK OF FAITH

100 STORIES OF FAITH

FROM ORDINARY PEOPLE LIKE YOU AND ME

N.D. COLE

FOREWORD BY **ERIC "E.T." THOMAS, PHD**

HOW TO
CONNECT WITH N.D.

SUBSCRIBE TO THE ND500 PODCAST

Find the podcast on Apple Podcasts, iHeart Radio, Google Play, Spotify, Stitcher, Radio.com, or your favorite podcast provider.

VISIT THE WEBSITE

 www.ndcole.com

FOLLOW N.D. ON SOCIAL MEDIA

 facebook.com/ndcoleministries

 @ndcole

 @ndcole

The Book of Faith: 100 Stories of Faith from Ordinary People Like You and Me

© 2019 by N.D. Cole. All rights reserved.

ISBN: 978-1-7337253-0-9

Thomas & Johnson Publishing is committed to publishing works of quality and integrity. In that spirit, we are proud to offer this book to our readers; however, the stories, the experiences, and words are from the author as they were voluntarily shared.

Printed in the United States of America.

For more about author N.D. Cole, please visit *www.ndcole.com*

TABLE OF CONTENTS

FINANCES

"My husband & I lost nearly
everything, but our faith in
Christ pulled us through"
ROSALIND LEE
Sugar Land, Texas

"Christ strengthened me &
I made it through"
PATRICIA JOHNSON
Richmond, Texas

"It was like God sent two angels
to restore my health &
financial troubles"
JOE WILSON
Chicago, Illinois

"I went from nearly losing my
home to selling it for a profit"
KAM CHARLES
Converse, Texas

"God provided for my family when
we couldn't provide for ourselves"
CLARENCE WOODS
Eldorado, Arkansas

"I'm debt free"
LORETTA HENDRIX
Little Rock, Arkansas

DEATH

"My mom died in a car accident
when I was 17 years old, but I
was able to experience joy in
a bad situation"
BRANDON RICH
Plano, Texas

"I buried my husband on our 50th
wedding anniversary, but God…"
CONSTANCE SIMS
Atlanta, Georgia

"My son was killed in 1991, but
now I have Christ's peace that
surpasses all understanding"
DORIS WALLER
Holly Springs, Mississippi

"I grew in faith while caring for
both of my ailing parents"
RONALD WILLIAMS
Sugar Land, Texas

"When my mom died, I didn't
think I could make it, but with
God, I did"
PATRICIA BOGA
Holly Springs, Mississippi

"My mom's death was unbearable
until I gave it to God"
LEROY ROBERTS
Houston, Texas

COLLEGE

"The Lord made a way out of no way"

CALVIN CALEB
Prichard, Alabama

"By trusting God, I was able to get a college degree"

KAREN FOUNTAIN
Moss Point, Mississippi

"I was denied admission; but then out of nowhere, I was later accepted by the same university"

CHRISTINA TUCKER
Fayetteville, Georgia

"I was faced with paying $40,000 a year for my children to go to college & God made a way"

MICHAEL SAM
Houston, Texas

EMPLOYMENT & CAREER

"For trusting Him, God took me from administrative assistant to director"

PAMELA NETTER
New Orleans, Louisiana

"My faith in Christ turned a temporary position into 40 years of employment"

MARION DENISE FOX
Gautier, Mississippi

"Having faith & trusting God's timing has made the difference in my life"

SHARRON GOODMAN-HILL
Decatur, Mississippi

"Chaos was everywhere on my job, but obeying God's direction to stay still resulted in one of the biggest blessings of my life"

CLIFTON FRANKLIN
Gilbert, Louisiana

"Faith in Christ resulted in me having a blessed career"

FANNIE LAMPLEY
Holly Springs, Mississippi

"Coaching was a God-sent assignment for me"

HENRY T. HOOD
Holly Springs, Mississippi

"By trusting & listening to God, I was blessed with a new job"

ASHLEY PAYNE
Lithonia, Georgia

"I lost my job after 19 years of employment"

RICKY ALLEN JOHNSON
Moss Point, Mississippi

"I was a teen mom, but through faith, I've accomplished a lot"

ERICA STEWART
Prichard, Alabama

"I moved to another state with no job in order to pursue my dream career"

ERIC ELLIOT
Richmond, Texas

FOREWORD

"Faith is the substance of things hoped for,
the evidence of things not seen..."
HEBREWS 11:1

AS I READ THROUGH THESE STORIES OF HOPE AND FAITH, tragedy and triumph, I was genuinely moved. It was not so long ago that I too was on the "rough side of the mountain," and my faith—what little of it there was at the time—saw me through.

N.D. Cole has produced a tome that will not only touch the heart and mind of the reader, but more important, it will start a conversation that will change lives. No matter where you come from, who you are, or however many times you've failed, God's purpose for you will be fulfilled if you are willing to believe and move in faith.

If you're unsure what that looks like, I encourage you to read this book and let Cole's collected stories of faith and hope show you the way.

ERIC THOMAS, PH.D.
Founder & CEO,
Eric Thomas & Associates, LLC

DEDICATION

Dear Reader,

This book is dedicated to you. Before you were born, God planned *this* moment in your life. It is no accident that you're holding this book. God longs for you to discover the life He created you to live—here on earth, and forever in eternity. Getting there requires faith and your acceptance of his son, Jesus Christ as Lord and Savior.

Hebrews 11:6 says, *"But without faith it is impossible to please Him, for he who comes to God must believe that He is, and that He is a rewarder of those who diligently seek Him."*

I believe that fulfilling your ultimate purpose in life will require an act of faith on your part. I pray that the stories that follow empower you with not only the courage to step out on faith to fulfill your destiny, but also the confirmation that if God can perform miracles, healing, and restoration in the lives of others, He will most certainly do it for you too! Trust God and reap the reward that God promises.

May God bless you abundantly above all you can ask or think.

Sincerely,
N.D. COLE

ACKNOWLEDGMENTS

To my mother, Cynthia J. Cole and father, Ben T. Cole II, I thank you for all of your guidance, support, and encouragement to never give up on my dreams. It is because of you that I am the man I am today. To me, you're the greatest parents ever to live. Your stories of faith will encourage the people of God for generations to come. I consider this book to be my greatest professional accomplishment, and I thank you for instilling in me the drive and discipline to complete this project.

To my brothers, Ben Cole III, and Victor Cole. Both of you have been there for me whenever I needed you. We share a bond that can never be broken. I love both of you. I would also like to thank those who had a hand in raising me, past and present members of Hopewell #1 Baptist Church, teachers and administrators at C.A.D.E.T. Jr. High School, Bishop Byrne High School, and the faculty and staff at Rust College.

To my beautiful daughters, Zariah, and Mackenzi. I thank God for blessing me with the two of you. I could not imagine my life without you all. From the ups and downs we've shared as a family, the one thing that has remained constant, is the love you all show toward me. Thank you for being the best daughters a father could ever ask for and thank you for encouraging me while writing this book.

Lastly, my wife, Tawanna. You have always stood by me through thick and thin. Thank you for entertaining all of my unconventional business ideas, ventures, and aspirations to be the best that I can be. You push me to be better. You encourage me never to take anything less than what God has for me. From the moment I saw you singing in the choir at Union Baptist Church, I knew you were the one. Who knew that God would turn my trip to Walmart to grab a pack of hot dogs and a can of beans into my opportunity to introduce myself to you? You complete me. The things that I lack, God has gifted you with those attributes. Together, we are unstoppable. I look forward to growing old with you and ultimately spending eternity with you and our two daughters. I am confident that the best is yet to come.

INTRODUCTION

by N.D. Cole

MONDAY, OCTOBER 11, 2004, WAS THE WORST DAY OF MY LIFE. I remember it like it was yesterday. I was working as a news journalist for *The Sun Herald* newspaper in Gulfport, Mississippi. Everything was going well for me. I was a rising talent in the newspaper industry, and I had just written the best story of my career. I was engaged to the woman of my dreams—Tawanna McInnis. Everything was going according to the plan I made for myself. Then I received a phone call from my editor. It was my day off.

However, my editor asked me to come to his office, which was approximately 30 minutes away from where I lived in Pascagoula, Mississippi. Without hesitation, I said yes, I'll be there in less than an hour. I didn't know what he wanted, but the fact that I had just written the best story of my life via investigative reporting I had been working on for months, indicated that something good was about to happen.

In my mind, I thought my editor was going to give me a raise, a promotion, or both. Whatever it was, I was ready for it. But when I arrived in his office, my editor and his boss, the managing editor was in the room. We proceeded to walk to a private office, an office I had never seen before. We sat at a square table. The two of them sat on one side. I was at the other. We exchanged pleasantries, and then I heard words that I thought I would never hear in my life: we're going to have to let you go.

Stunned, shocked, and in total disbelief, I asked them why. What did I do? Why now? What about that great story I just wrote?

I never received a real explanation—at least one that I felt justified what just happened. Upset, I looked them both in the eyes and said, "you know that this is not right." I gave them my employee badge, walked out of the building, and called my father, who is an attorney. Boiling hot on the inside, I was ready to sue.

However, my father told me that in the state of Mississippi, employers don't have to provide a specific reason for termination. That meant that I was out of a job, and my plans to marry the woman of my dreams was in jeopardy. In an effort to "fix" my circumstances, I called everyone I knew with connections in the newspaper industry to help me find a new job. The result: No one was hiring.

You see, the internet was just starting to boom, and the newspaper industry was on a major decline in readership. Advertising revenue was down, and the future was uncertain. So here I was, a talented writer with no job and absolutely no savings in my bank account. Before this event, I would often "say" with my mouth that I had faith in God, but this was really the first time in my life in which I had to "show" that I had faith in God and that I trusted His plan for my life. Quite honestly, I didn't handle it too well. It felt like I lost everything I had worked for.

In fact, I was so upset with God that during a testimonial period during Wednesday night Bible study at Union Baptist Church in Pascagoula, Mississippi, I walked to the front of the church, grabbed the microphone, and said, "I've been sitting here listening to all of your testimonies about how good God is and how He doesn't fail. Well, the truth is that God does fail because He failed me."

I will never forget the response. An older lady whom I really respected, Ms. Clem, got up and told me, "baby, you may think God has failed you, but He has not failed you. In time you will see."

Time went on, and after an entire year of being angry with God and fighting His plan, I just gave up and told God that I would sweep floors if I had to. I just needed a job. A few days later. I received an offer. But it was a job that most people in the area avoid—the FedEx World Hub in Memphis, Tennessee. Jokes and analogies are often made about the Memphis Hub saying they work you like a Hebrew slave there. But I was familiar with this type of work. It was the same job I had while I was in college. I went from being a professional journalist to throwing boxes in 100 plus degree summer heat and 10-degree winter weather, all the while having to explain to all of my friends why I was back at home living with my mother and father. This was an humbling experience, but I was happy to be at work. I worked that job like I had never worked before. I showed up early, stayed late when asked, and simply gave my all to it.

After a few months, God opened another door: it was a job as a writer at a marketing and advertising company in Memphis. Now I had two jobs: FedEx at night and this new position as a writer in a field I had never worked in before. And get this: the owner of the company really liked me, so he took me under his wing to show me the ends and outs of marketing as well as business. That eventually led to an opportunity to start my own business writing advertising copy for businesses across the globe.

You see, while I was in the newspaper industry, I was doing well, but I really wanted something more. However, I was too afraid to step out and do it. God knew this too, so He forced me into a new season, but it required faith and trust on my part. And that's what this book is all about.

I remember my father telling me about the time he had to trust God when he was accepted into a law school in Iowa, but did not have anywhere to stay. I thought to myself, what if there was a book of encouragement that profiled the stories of faith from ordinary people from across the country, who just like my father and I, had to step out on faith and trust God—a modern version of Hebrews 11 in the Bible, known as the Hall of Faith. This chapter profiles the patriarchs of faith, such as Abraham and Noah, who had to step out on faith and trust God. I thought about writing this book for years, and in 2016, God spoke to me and said, "It's time. Write the book."

After more than a year of interviewing, writing, re-writing, editing, and re-editing, I completed the assignment God gave me. I titled it, *The Book of Faith: 100 Stories of Faith from Ordinary People Like You and Me."*

It is my prayer that the stories that follow encourage you and empower you with hope during your walk of faith. And by the way, the woman of my dreams that I spoke about earlier— she stood by me, and God allowed me to marry her on July 14, 2007. Today, we are blessed beyond measure with two daughters, a loving home, and a puppy named Coco.

CHAPTER 1
STARTING A BUSINESS

HURRICANE KATRINA WAS
A BLESSING IN DISGUISE

When most people think of a hurricane, potential destruction and disaster come to mind, but for one Richmond, Texas resident, it took a hurricane for him to receive his ultimate blessing in life.

Darrick Brown was one of the thousands forced to leave homes in New Orleans and start their lives over in Texas when Hurricane Katrina slammed the Gulf Coast in 2005.

Brown said leaving the only city he had ever called home was one of the hardest decisions he's ever made, but noted that it was his faith in God that gave him the courage and strength to lead his family down an unknown path.

"To leave my city was devastating to me," he said.

More than a decade later, as it turns out, the hurricane was a blessing for Brown and his family. Brown realized his dream of owning his own barbershop after moving to Richmond, Texas, just south of Houston. He owns and operates Thirty-II-Degreez Barber Shop at 14800 Westheimer on Houston's west side.

"My business is steadily growing day by day," he said. "I never thought leaving New Orleans would land me the success that I am encountering now as a barber here in the state of Texas."

Brown, who lost virtually everything that he owned during Katrina, said life after the storm has been great and says he owes it all to the almighty God that he serves.

"I have a beautiful home, my wife has a real nice job, my younger son is getting a very good education, and we are putting my oldest son, Matthew, through college," he said. "Blessings have been constantly poured upon my family and I."

Brown said his barbershop is thriving at a time when many businesses are closing because of the poor economy.

"Here in my shop, I have a total of 12 booths," he said. "At the moment, I have 11 booths filled with certified barbers. I'm looking to hire a hair braider and two hair stylists."

Brown said Hurricane Katrina and its aftermath had taught him much about dealing with personal problems.

"I have always been one who rolls with the flow, meaning, if a wave comes, I flow with the wave instead of fighting against it," he said. He added that being able to adapt to whatever life throws your way is important.

"It's true that Katrina and being forced to move west was very challenging, but I had to quickly adapt to this life-changing experience," Brown said. "At the beginning, I was scared, but then the surviving family man quickly appeared. Decisions had to be made and made quickly. This specific time in my life was a definite walk of faith for me. I am a testimony to what God can do through you if you just have faith and trust Him."

BY FAITH, MY DREAM DEFERRED CAME TRUE

DANIEL S. BROWN
Houston, Texas

When Daniel Brown walked into a meeting with his boss in 2015, he knew it wasn't going to be an ordinary meeting. As the head of HR for BP Western Hemisphere, this would be the same conversation that he had given many times to others saying the company was transitioning to a new model. Now, it was his turn to hear it, because this time, it was his position that was being eliminated.

"The day before I was on top of the world," Brown recalled. "Quite honestly, I felt that life couldn't get any better for me. I really felt like there was nothing in the world that wasn't possible. I was happy with my marriage, happy with my job, happy with my daughter and family. However, the very next day, my boss had flown over from London, and we had a meeting. In that meeting, she told me that my job was being moved to London, and I had an opportunity apply for roles in the U.S., but there was no guarantee or assurance that I would have a job."

I was making about a half a million dollars a year, and my job being eliminated rocked me to my core...

Brown, a husband, and father of a young daughter, all of a sudden had a new set of circumstances on his hands, circumstances in which he says only his faith in God could solve. After speaking with his wife, Brown decided to take a bold step of faith.

I decided to pursue my dream of being a business owner...

"Immediately I concluded that opening a State Farm Insurance Agency was the way to go because I've always respected the organization and the investment they make to assist agents in succeeding," Brown said, before adding, "I went through test after test just to get onto the consideration slate."

Brown said although he could not see what the outcome of stepping out on faith to pursue his dream of being a business owner would be, he says he was confident in what God could do.

"Instead of having anxiety about it, I decided to look at it another way, saying to myself that if I trust the Lord the way that I say I trust Him, I should trust Him now," Brown said. "This was a dream deferred in my eyes. I placed my faith in Him, and it seemed like everything just fell into place."

On April 1, 2016, the doors of my State Farm Agency opened...

"Looking back at my decision, I can say that this was the right decision," Brown said. "I credit this to having faith in God. One of the things that I see is that I haven't had the struggles that some agents have gone through. It's not easy, but things seemed to have just fallen into place. I'm grateful to be able to do this, and I encourage others to follow their dreams through faith too."

Daniel Brown's State Farm Insurance Agency is located at 2121 Sage Rd #190, Houston, TX 77056, and you can find his insurance agency's website at *www.dbinsuresme2.com*.

I STARTED WITH A BUCKET, A LAMP, ONE FOLDING CHAIR & FAITH

JOHN "JOE BLACK" BROWN
New Orleans, Louisiana

John Brown has always wanted to own his very own barbershop, but it took a bold act of faith during unfavorable circumstances that brought his dream to reality.

"I moved to Houston, Texas due to Hurricane Katrina in 2005," Brown said. "I came to Houston on a voluntary evacuation having plans to go back to New Orleans after spending a weekend, but low and behold, Hurricane Katrina came and hit New Orleans, and I couldn't go back."

Having lost everything that they owned in New Orleans, Brown, his wife, and son, all of a sudden found themselves having to live in a city in which they didn't know anything about.

"This was my family's first time ever coming to Houston, so we were lost, we didn't know anybody here," Brown recalled. "We were just fending for ourselves and trying to find our way, but God had directions for that."

With no means to provide for himself and his family, Brown said he started looking for employment to support his family.

"I went to the store and got me some pants, a polo shirt, brown shoes, and started looking for a job," Brown said. "I didn't know where I was going, so I started driving, and took the first exit that said downtown Houston. I had never been to Houston, so I was lost. I came upon a street where there was a barbershop that was open. It was a Monday. I went into the barbershop, and they told me that they didn't have anything. They referred me to another barbershop that was on the other end of town. I went there, and nothing was available, so I went home to try to figure something out."

Before becoming a professional barber, Brown said he worked at a restaurant in New Orleans, which provided him with restaurant-related skills, so his second option was to look for work at a restaurant. However, that option didn't work either, because another storm was brewing in the Gulf of Mexico, but this time it was headed for Houston.

"Hurricane Rita came to Houston, so everybody had to evacuate from Houston," Brown said. "I evacuated from Katrina in New Orleans to Houston, and now evacuations were happening from Hurricane Rita in Houston. After we evacuated from Hurricane Rita, I got a phone call from one of the barbershops I visited when I first came to Houston. They told me that one of their barbers evacuated from Hurricane Rita to San Antonio and didn't come back, so this was my opportunity to work at a barbershop. I accepted the offer, and I worked there for a year and a half."

I decided it was time for me to branch out on my own, so I went out on faith...

"I didn't have much to start a business," Brown stressed, before adding, "I only had $2,000 in my bank account and faith. I drove around, not knowing where I was going. It was all on faith. I drove down Martin Luther King Street and saw a building that was for lease. I called the number, and the landlord answered and said he would meet me at 3 o'clock. We met at 3 o'clock; we opened the door, the walls were green, the floor was blue and had smut on it from some kind of smoke. You really couldn't tell the true color of the floors. I looked at the layout of it and said, you know what, this is me. I saw beyond the walls and the floor."

Brown noted that before the landlord told him how much the lease was, he had already made it up in his mind that he was going to take it. Internally, Brown was praying that the lease would be something he could afford.

"When he gave me the numbers, I said, ok, I'm going to make it happen," Brown recalled. "I stood there and started cleaning up after we signed the papers. After that, I went to Home Depot and bought some cleaning supplies. Again, I only had $2,000, so I had to stretch this. I was doing the majority of the work on my own. I got a guy that was standing outside of Home Depot that does painting work, so I asked him if he would be willing to help for a small amount of money. He came with me back to the shop, and we started painting the walls. We painted the walls until we both were tired. I continued working to do things for the shop on my own because I didn't have money to pay people to do it for me. I started buying cabinets and things, not knowing who was going to put them up, or if I had to put them up myself by watching YouTube videos, or something like that.

On April 1, 2008, I opened Joe Black Barbershop...

Brown said he started calling the customers he gained while working at the previous barbershop.

"I asked them if they wanted to get their haircut," Brown said. "I told them that I didn't have actual barber chairs, but I had a bucket that I can cut your hair and I have electricity, so they started coming. I am very grateful for my clients, because they went on this journey with me, and they are still my clients today. I started cutting their hair on a bucket and a cooler. Every penny I made, I put back into my barbershop. We evolved, and now I am here by the grace of God. Without Him, I promise you this would not have happened, because I didn't know where I was going. My family and I, we were lost, we didn't have anything.

Today, Joe Black Barbershop has a total of seven barbers, and a manicure and pedicure for men only located inside of the barbershop to accommodate men who don't want to go to a nail salon for a manicure and pedicure.

"This is through the grace of God that everything that I've been through, losing everything, and here I am still going strong, and knowing that God isn't through with me yet," Brown said. "I can testify that by stepping out on faith and trusting God even if you don't have anything, or know which direction to go, your life will be blessed."

As a result of having faith in God to make a dream a reality, Houston Mayor Sylvester Turner, on behalf of the city of Houston, signed a proclamation declaring September 6, 2017, Joe Black Barbershop Day. Joe Black Barbershop is located at 6516 Broadway St. Suite 140, Pearland, TX 77581. Its website address is *www.joeblackbarbershop.com*.

"I LEFT MY FULL-TIME JOB WITH BENEFITS TO START MY OWN ORGANIZATION

MARCIE BROOKS
Houston, Texas

Marcie Brooks has always had a passion for helping high school students apply for college and secure scholarships. She loved doing it so much that the thought of doing it full-time entered her mind. Like most people, the realities of life and responsibilities of providing for her family and paying bills also entered her mind, but she says it was through her faith in God that gave her the courage to step out on faith and do what she truly loved to do.

"I started a non-profit organization called Academia In Motion (A.I.M.) in 2009," Brooks said. "I started working with kids on the weekends while I was working my full-time job in the communications department at Texas Southern University. People started referring kids, and it started to grow. But in 2013, my mom died. I live in Houston, and my mom was buried in St. Louis. On my way back from the funeral in St. Louis, I started thinking that life is too short, so why not go ahead and go full-time?"

As a result:

I submitted my two-week notice, and I haven't looked back...

Brooks said the thought of leaving a full-time job with benefits was something to really think about, but she says the only thing she could do is place her faith in Christ to see her through it all.

"I went full-time in 2014," Brooks said. "My mom actually came up with the name of my organization. I have gone through some challenges, but it has been the best decision I could have ever made."

A.I.M. was awarded the Super Bowl Grant, and now I have a salary...

Brooks noted that funding is a crucial element in starting an organization or business, so she started writing grants to help with funding for her organization. The Super Bowl was held in Houston in February 2017, and there was a Super Bowl grant opportunity.

Touchdown Houston, a charitable giving program created by the Houston Super Bowl Host Committee in partnership with the NFL Foundation, gave $4 million in grants to 78 local and non-profit organizations within the 11 counties of Houston. The grants concentrated on three key areas: education, health, and community enhancement. The grants were administered through the Greater Houston Community Foundation, the official administrator of the Touchdown Houston Charitable Fund. The NFL Foundation contributed $1 million.

"I met with the people and started working on the grant," Brooks said, "It was the second grant that I had written and thanks to God, A.I.M. was awarded the grant. It's our biggest grant award to date, and I am able to get a salary from the grant. I'm glad that I had the faith to step out on faith and trust that God would bless my decision to leave my full-time job with benefits in order to do A.I.M. full-time. I'm so glad that I did because none of this would have been possible had I not stepped out on faith and trusted in God's plan."

A.I.M. is an educational consulting company that provides strategic advising for students considering colleges, universities, and graduate programs that results in a higher percentage of successful admissions, scholarships, and awards for students. A.I.M.'s mission is to promote the value of learning, self-worth among students and families, quality performance, and transition for students to productive and responsible participation in society.

A.I.M.'s website is *academiainmotion.com.*

BY HAVING THE FAITH OF A MUSTARD SEED, MY DREAM OF OPENING MY OWN PEDIATRICS CLINIC CAME TRUE

CHARLENE JOHNSON BROWN
Fayetteville, Georgia

Dr. Charlene Johnson Brown always dreamed of one day having her own pediatrics clinic, but she says her dream became a reality in a way in which she could never have imagined, and she credits it all to having the faith of a mustard seed in Christ to set everything in motion.

Brown, a 1996 graduate of Morehouse School of Medicine, specializing in pediatrics, said she had been working for a doctor in Atlanta from 2001 to 2006 when she decided that she wanted to open up her own clinic.

"We had a dispute, and there was talk of cutting my pay, meaning I would make $10,000 to $15, 000 less than I was already making," Brown recalled. "I said to myself that there had to be something better for me, so I decided to leave and journey out on my own to start my own clinic."

But there was a huge problem: I couldn't get a loan anywhere, and all I had was $1,500 in my bank account, which was much less than my monthly bills, so I didn't even know how I was going to make it...

Brown said all she could do is pray to God for help. As a wife and mother of a young daughter, she says she was out of options and needed a miracle. Brown added that although she was getting turned down for loans, in the back of her mind, she was also wondering to herself how she would even be able to run a clinic without any experience running a clinic, in addition to having no staff, and no money in order to pay the staff.

"I received a call from a guy who I met three years prior," Brown said, before adding, "He was over a program where international students come for residency in America."

He told me that a doctor all of a sudden died of a heart attack and that this already established medical clinic needed someone to come in and take it over. I took the opportunity, and I ended up with not one, but two clinics…

"What made it so sweet is that there was a person already working in the clinic who had years of experience running a clinic and she told me not to worry about anything and that she would work for free for three months," Brown said. "Then, keep in mind that I didn't have any money, so even with a clinic, I had to pay rent for the building, but I was told by the people who owned the building that I didn't have to pay any rent for three months."

It blew my mind, because everything that I was worried about, God had already put everything in place; He was just waiting on me to step out on faith and trust Him…

Brown noted that her entire life, she heard her mother, father, and various others of the Christian faith quote the Bible verse, "Because of your unbelief; for assuredly, I say to you, if you have faith as a mustard seed, you will say to this mountain, 'Move from here to there,' and it will move; and nothing will be impossible for you (Matthew 17:20).'"

"I never understood that verse until I went through this," Brown said. "I'm a witness that the only thing you have to do is have just a small piece of faith. You don't need much, just trust Him, and He will work things out for you. I'm a witness that all things work together for the good of those who love the Lord and are called to His purpose. Look at what He did for me. When God gives you something, He gives it to you. You won't have to worry about anything. He'll bless you, but it all starts and ends with faith."

Dr. Charlene Johnson Brown owns Camp Creek Pediatrics in Atlanta. Her website is *www.campcreekpediatrics.com*.

I JUMPED & GOD CAUGHT ME

JOY MEDLEY

St. Elizabeth Parish, Jamaica

For many people, unfavorable circumstances are what keeps them from moving forward in life, but for Joy Medley, unfavorable circumstances are what allowed her to do what she really wanted to do in life: own her own business and be the first in her family to receive a master's degree.

"I struggled my way through college as a single mom," Medley recalled. "After graduating from college in 1999, I looked for a job in my field of study, but I couldn't find any. Having a child, I could not afford to wait for a job in my field, so I took a job through a friend. The job was completely outside of the field in which I studied, but the job had good benefits. It was stable, and I needed to feed my child, so I took it. However, I kind of got stuck there, because I wasn't getting any experience in my field of study."

And before she knew it, over a decade had gone by since she had taken the job. Her son, who was five years old when she started working the job, was now graduating from college.

"I started to pray because I really felt trapped," Medley said. "God kept telling me to just leave and pursue what He was telling me to pursue, which was to start a cleaning business, but in my heart, I also wanted to go to grad school."

I was really in a state of misery. I couldn't leave the job, but I wanted to leave the job, but I didn't know where I would go. I kept asking God, you said move, but where am I going to move to?

"I kept saying, 'God, you already know the situation. If I leave this job, we don't eat, and He kept saying you need to trust me,'" Medley said, before adding, "One day a customer whom I dealt with every month walked into the office. It just so happened that he was having trouble getting people to carry out the work for his cleaning company. Although I had dealt with this customer every month, I never knew he had a cleaning company. We talked, and he subcontracted some cleaning work out to me. And as soon as he did that, I just felt like God was saying this is your open door. Go to it and trust me."

God just kept saying jump...

"Even though the money I was being paid working this subcontract was not what I was making on the job that I wanted to leave, I did jump. I left the job that I wanted to leave, and within two or three months of me doing that, I picked up a commercial contract for myself," Medley said. "This contract was totally mine, and I was making twice the amount of money I was making at that company I wanted to leave."

I had to hire some people, and the business started taking off...

But God's favor didn't stop there.

"I had applied to the University of Maryland months before I took that jump, that leap of faith on the cleaning business," Medley recalled. "I ended up getting into graduate school. God gave me the two things I really wanted: my own business, it's called Cleaning Medley, and being able to attend graduate school."

Medley said her walk of faith is a testimony to others that trusting and having faith in Christ is the best thing anyone could ever do.

What I had to do is listen to God, but I went through three years of misery trying to figure out what God was going to do when all I needed to do was have faith that whatever He does, it's going to work out for my good...

"Looking back on everything, I can see how I learned so much from the entire event," Medley said. "Blind faith is a good thing because if you try to figure out what God is going to do, you will never really do what He wants you to do."

Medley graduated from the University of Maryland Online College in the spring of 2018 with a master's degree in distance and online education.

IT TOOK ME 30 YEARS TO STEP OUT ON FAITH

JAMES DONALD
Houston, Texas

Stepping out on faith to fulfill his ultimate purpose in life is something that didn't come easy for James Donald. In fact, it took several decades of living the life that "he" thought he wanted for himself before he accepted the life that God had predestined.

"I was really deep in the world," Donald stressed. "I was into some of everything, drugs, everything. Another guy and I were just into a lot of not so good things."

Donald, however, noted that he knew he had a calling on his life.

"I had a call to do God's work," Donald said. "It wasn't until I went to see a play called Heaven or Hell when I gave my life to Christ. In the year of 1993, I started my calling to preach. Ever since then, God has been really, really good."

Donald went on to point out that had he continued to sell himself short by "not" accepting what God had planned for him, he never would have met his wife of 22 years, and he would never have been the father of his son and daughter.

"Had I not stepped out on faith, I would not have had the courage to start my own business either," said Donald, owner of Donald Enterprises, which specializes in tax preparation and providing community mentorship programs.

"We mentor and everything," Donald said of the company which launched in 2016. "God has been taking care of us. I came out of a lifestyle where I was really in the world of sin, and God brought me out of that sin. Now I'm saved. I preach and teach the Word of God. My life is a testimony to someone who is living the lifestyle opposite of what God has called them to be.

Not knowing what's in the future is part of the process, but when you place your total faith and trust in God, your life will be blessed. I went from having drug money to having legit money. The blessing is that as soon as I accepted the life that God had for me, the guy that I was running with got arrested and went to prison. Had I continued not doing what God had called me to do, I would have been in prison too. Stepping out on faith was a real faith and trust walk for me. It took me 30 years to step out on faith, but I'm so glad that I did."

CHAPTER 2
SPORTS

PLAYER OF THE GAME

ZARIAH MCINNIS

10 POINTS
4-4 FIELD GOAL

"
I ONLY HAD A 1% CHANCE
OF RECEIVING A COLLEGE
BASKETBALL SCHOLARSHIP,
BUT I TRUSTED GOD
& IT WORKED

ZARIAH MCINNIS
Sugar Land, Texas

When Zariah McInnis was just five years old, it was obvious to those around her that she had a natural gift of playing basketball. That gift ignited a dream of hers to one day earn a scholarship to play college basketball, something that, according to NCAA statistics, only one to three percent of more than 435,885 high school girls basketball players in America have the chance to experience.

For many athletes and parents, playing select/AAU sports is seen as the best way to get a scholarship. But while playing AAU, McInnis noticed a huge problem: she was no longer attending church on a regular basis. The basketball season was long and the time commitment that's required to participate seemed even longer to her.

In fact, the AAU season starts each year at the end of February and lasts until the end of July. McInnis had tournaments in and out of town on Friday nights, two to three games on Saturdays, and also games on Sundays. This was in addition to two, 2½- hour practices during the school week. In short, by playing AAU basketball, the church would no longer fit into her schedule. It meant that she had to stop attending Sunday church services on a regular basis for six to seven months out of the year.

Her solution: "I really wanted a scholarship to play college basketball, but…"

As an act of faith, I gave up AAU basketball in order to keep God first in my Life…

"Before I started playing AAU my family and I attended church and served God every Sunday, and we also attended Wednesday night Bible study," said McInnis, who was also a member of the church choir and usher ministry. "I sat down with my parents, and we realized that with practicing several times a week for 2½ hours at a time and playing games in and out of town nearly every week that I was actually putting basketball first in my life and not God. My dad, who is a minister, always recited Matthew 6:33, "But seek first the kingdom of God and His righteousness, and all these things shall be added to you."

McInnis decided to go on faith and trust that God would open a door for her at the right time.

"Many of my friends thought I was crazy for making this decision because playing AAU in Texas, generally speaking, is seen as a way of life, or the only way to get a scholarship," McInnis said. "It was hard seeing many of my friends who continued to play AAU to start receiving interest from colleges while I seemingly went unnoticed from the sixth grade and all throughout high school."

But during her 12th-grade year, several colleges took notice of McInnis from a social media profile she and her dad set up in August 2016. Each morning and evening, McInnis posted short clips of her doing basketball drills on Twitter and Instagram in hopes of catching the eye of a college scout.

"Most players who play college basketball make a verbal commitment during their junior year, so here I was a senior with literally no interest until we set up a profile," McInnis said. "Most colleges were done recruiting by this time, but God opened up a door. I was invited to two college visits."

On April 11, 2017, I signed a scholarship to play college basketball at the University of St. Thomas in Houston, Texas...

"Only one percent of high school athletes get the opportunity to play college basketball," McInnis stressed, before adding,

"Not playing AAU drastically decreases the already slim chances of receiving a college basketball scholarship, but God rewarded me for having faith in Him and trusting Him. I am a living witness that God is able to make what man says is impossible, possible."

WITH GOD, MY DREAM OF PLAYING IN THE NFL CAME TRUE

DANIEL CLARK IV
Country Club Hills, Illinois

When Daniel Clark was a child, his dream was to play professional football. However, he was always told that he was too skinny, too slow, and too unknown, but by the grace of God, his life-long dream came true.

"In high school, I was a three-sport athlete competing in football, basketball, and baseball. One might assume that I was some athletic Phenom, but that was not the case," Clark said. "From my perspective, I was an average athlete at best. In regards to my future aspirations, my parents were second-generation postal workers, so I fixed my eyes on continuing that legacy by becoming the third generation to work for the United States Postal Service. At the time, no one in my family had ever completed college, so I did not have a deep-seated desire to pursue a secondary education."

Though, I played three different sports in high school; my true passion was for the game of football...

"From a physical aspect, my stature did not necessarily align with my desire to participate in such a violent game," Clark said. "As a two-way player (Quarterback/Linebacker), I was a tall, scrawny kid with bowed-legs and slewed feet. Honestly, I looked pretty awkward in my uniform. I was not the fastest nor the strongest kid on my team, let alone in the conference, state, or country. However, the one thing that the Lord did bless me with is the heart of a lion. On the football field, I was blessed with an innate sense of resilience, or the never quit attitude. After a productive junior football season in high school, I still did not receive any recognition by the experts on the state or national level. This was just the reality check that I needed to reassess my expectations of becoming a third-generation postal worker."

But then God showed up...

"That summer (July 1995), one of my teammates invited a few players and me to attend and compete in a 7-on-7 passing tournament at the University of Illinois Urban-Champaign," Clark said. "Our team ended up competing in the championship game. As you may know that the QB gets the blame when your team loses, but they also get the credit when you win. Though I got the credit for the success of our team, it was no one but God who got the glory for what happened next:

At the conclusion of that camp, the Head Coach, Lou Tepper, called me into his office and offered me a full scholarship to attend the University of Illinois-Urbana...

"I humbly accepted his offer while fully understanding that this opportunity was presented to me only by the grace of God," Clark stressed, before adding, "After graduating high school, I arrived on campus as a 189-pound unknown QB, who had not been recognized at the state or national level until I had committed to the University of Illinois the previous summer. Within a week or so, my position was changed to defensive back, something I had never played before.

Nevertheless, I embrace the opportunity to compete on the scout team as a freshman. Division I institutions customarily have an abundance of resources to assist in bulking up its players to better equip them for competition in intercollegiate athletics. I was a prime candidate who greatly benefited from those particular resources. The Lord blessed me to gain 22 pounds of muscle in a little over a year's time. In addition, an injury to a childhood friend and teammate allowed my position to move once again from defense back/safety to linebacker. Not in my wildest dreams did I ever imagine I could ever compete as a linebacker at a Division I major college football program, but the Lord had a different plan and purpose for my life."

I finished my college career at No. 6 on the all-time tackle leader chart in school history with 384, one spot above Hall of Fame Linebacker Dick Butkus...

Clark noted that he believes that just like Jesus healed the sick, caused the blind to see, and raised the dead, God allowed him to play major college football and is still performing miracles today.

"Not only did He bless me to be the first in my family to attend a four-year university, but also to earn a Bachelors Degree in Speech Communications," Clark said. "At the age of 9, I began playing the game of football. I had dreams of playing at the highest level, but I never expected that it could ever be a possibility."

I was picked 245th in the 7th round of 2000 NFL Draft by the Jacksonville Jaguars...

Clark stressed that generally, a seventh-round pick does not have a favorable chance of making the team or completing an entire training camp for that matter.

"However, the Lord blessed me to play 12 years with five different organizations (Jaguars, Raiders, Saints, Texans, and Giants)," Clark said. "There is no way this journey was possible outside of God's divine will. He orchestrated this plan for His majestic glory. As for my story of faith, our Lord and Savior

Jesus Christ says it best, "With men this is impossible, but with God all things are possible."

Clark retired from the NFL in 2011. Today, he serves as a minister of the Gospel.

"
I LEARNED TO TRUST HIS WILL AFTER MY NFL DREAM DIDN'T COME TRUE

JASON B. MONTANEZ
Brooklyn, New York

Ever since Jason Montanez was a little kid, he wanted to play in the NFL, but an injury on the day before his NFL tryout forever changed the trajectory of his life. However, he credits his faith in Christ for providing him with more blessings than he believes he would have ever received playing in the NFL.

"For you to work so hard for something and it not pan out in your favor, it's a hard pill to swallow," Montanez said.

Montanez' story goes back to 1999, his freshman year of college. He had a desire to one day play in the NFL. However, he didn't have a football scholarship, but instead of quitting, he decided to try out as a walk-on for the football team at the University of Buffalo.

"Through my faith, I continued to work hard and move up the ranks, which was a blessing to me," Montanez said, before adding, "However, the coaches that year got fired, and new coaches came in. I wasn't necessarily given a chance by the previous coaching staff where I played as a walk-on, but within six months of the new coaches arrival, I had gone from the scout team to having a starting position playing linebacker and fullback. I was awarded a full scholarship for the remainder of my playing career, the last two years."

Coaches were telling me that I had a shot at playing in the NFL...

"I was working very, very hard toward this particular goal of playing in the NFL, and the day before my tryout, which is called the pro day, I severely tore my hamstring running a 40-yard dash," Montanez recalled. "I immediately went into a panic.

The first thing that I questioned is, God why have you forsaken me? Why did this happen to me? Because of my injury, I tested very poorly, and I was never really able to recuperate from that particular injury."

What made Montanez' injury so hard to take is the fact that throughout his playing career, he had never sustained an injury.

"Just imagine the timing of this particular injury, and it was a non-contact injury too," Montanez said. "I got angry in a sense. For two or three years after this injury, my life was just a world spin. There was a point in my life where I stopped praying. I turned to alcohol for comfort, but by the grace of God I still decided to get my education, and I graduated with two bachelor degrees."

Montanez went on to stress that not realizing his dream of playing in the NFL was one of the hardest things he had to accept, simply because of the amount of time and effort he put into realizing his dream.

"All I could do is place my faith in God, to trust that He knew what was best for me, and as it turns out, He did know what was best for me," Montanez said. "It was the birth of my firstborn son, Jordan. That's when I realized that I had to shape up, that God is great, that God is good. There was a life that I was now responsible for that completely changed my outlook. I quickly understood that although playing in the NFL was my plan, and what I wanted, that was not the plan that God had for me."

Montanez noted that had he played in the NFL, he doesn't believe he would have the blessing of having a son today, nor had the opportunity to meet the countless people he has met, in addition to the relationships he has built along the way to founding his own leadership consulting firm.

"I chose to look at it from the perspective that I basically relinquished control," Montanez stressed. "I said, God, let your will be done, and I'm perfectly fine with it. That's a prayer I say every day. Let your will be done, and whatever your will is, I'll be ok with it. I've been in corporate America now for 15-16 years. I've been very successful, and by the grace of God, those experiences of hurt and disappointment, I feel that I have the tools and the skill set to conquer anything that life throws at me. By placing your faith in God, despite your circumstances, anyone else can conquer anything that life throws their way too. That's my testimony of faith."

CHAPTER 3
DREAMS

I WAS TOLD I WOULD NEVER GET PUBLISHED, BUT THROUGH FAITH, MY BOOK HAS SOLD ALL OVER THE WORLD

MARGAREE KING-MITCHELL
Kansas City, Kansas

When Margaree King-Mitchell's son came home sad one day in 1989 because he didn't have any grandparents to bring to grandparents day at school, she had no idea that God would use that episode to propel her to publish her first book, *Uncle Jed's Barbershop*—while also teaching her that through faith in Christ, all things are possible even if you don't have any connections in the book publishing industry, or know anybody who does.

"I tried to explain to him that both of his grandfathers had died before he was born, and because his living grandmothers lived in different cities that his grandparents wouldn't be able to come," Mitchell recalled, before adding, "He continued to be sad for about a month."

In an attempt to help solve the problem, Mitchell said she went to the library to find a picture book that was set in history, books that would help her son see and know what it was like for his ancestors to live in the South. She couldn't find any, so she decided to write one herself.

"When I had the concept, I went for a walk, and it was like God gave me the story to write," Mitchell noted. "I wrote the story, and I tried to get it published. I bought this book called the Children's Writers and Illustrators Market, and it had the names and addresses of publishers to send your book to consider for publication."

Mitchell, believing in the vision for her book that God gave her, wrote the book, and started sending off her story to publishers. She eagerly waited for a response, but...

I would get rejection letters...

"And the first rejection letter I got, I was just crushed because I knew that there were no books like that out there and I just felt that God had told me to write this book even though I had never written a book in my life," Mitchell said. "When I got my first rejection letter, I put the story away in a drawer, and I didn't send it out to anyone else."

After approximately four months had passed, Mitchell came across the story she wrote tucked away in the drawer. She took hold of her manuscript, encouraged herself, and sent it off again.

"I got another rejection letter," Mitchell recalled, "So back in the drawer my story went, and it stayed in the drawer another two or three months until I had built up enough courage to take it out and send it off again. This kept up for a couple of years; me putting my story away and getting up enough courage to take it out again."

Mitchell said she then started telling people about how she was trying to get her book published.

I remember that there was no encouragement...

"A lot of friends laughed at me and said you're never going to get your book published because you don't live in New York and you don't know anybody in the publishing industry," Mitchell said. "People were telling me to just forget about it. People were telling me that I might as well go and do something else because nobody is going to publish your book. But they had never even read my book, and they were telling me that nobody would publish it. I was crushed, and for a while, I listened to my friends, and I didn't send my story out anymore. I kept saying, 'God I know you gave me this story and I know you want it published and nobody is publishing it.'"

But then Mitchell decided to stop thinking small. She decided to go big. She zeroed in on book publisher Simon &

Schuster, one of the largest book publishing companies in existence. Simon & Schuster at the time was telling all prospective authors that they were not accepting stories unless an agent sent it to them or it came from someone that Simon & Schuster already knew and recommended it.

"Even though they said they weren't accepting manuscripts, I just sent it anyway," Mitchell said. "I just think it was God telling me to just send it in and see what happens. I had nothing to lose, and within two weeks, I received a call from an editor at Simon & Schuster saying that they wanted to publish my story."

That year (1993), Simon & Schuster, according to Mitchell, had a full roster of well-established authors, who were featured in a catalog in which the company published each year to advertise their new books for the year.

"Nobody knew me," she said. "I'm this new person, but my book, *Uncle Jed's Barbershop*, had the whole front and back cover. It was one continuous cover on the catalog. Then when you open the catalog, my book had a whole page inside the catalog. To me, that was nothing but God, because nobody knew me."

Uncle Jed's Barbershop took off. The book was featured on Reading Rainbow, it was in schools, in bookstores all across the country, as well as in several countries.

"When you trust God and go on faith, just so many good things happen," Mitchell said. "It was letting me know that I didn't need a person advocating for me when I had God advocating for me. And year after year after year, *Uncle Jed's Barbershop* has continued to sell. It has been reprinted in social studies textbooks, English and language arts textbooks, and the Federal Reserve Bank has developed lesson plans from my book. It has been sold in foreign markets, and all across the world."

But that's not all: an award-winning musical has been produced based on *Uncle Jed's Barbershop*.

"If you trust in God and believe when He tells you to do something, just do it, go for it," Mitchell stressed. "You may not know how it's going to come to pass, or what great things are going to happen because you stepped out on faith, but if you just trust Him, you never know. It may be like *Uncle Jed's Barbershop* and go around the world."

“I HAD NO MONEY & NO PLACE TO STAY ENTERING LAW SCHOOL, BUT BY TRUSTING GOD, I ACCOMPLISHED MY DREAM OF BECOMING AN ATTORNEY

BEN T. COLE II
Holly Springs, Mississippi

A s a young boy, Ben T. Cole II always dreamed of one day becoming an attorney, but for most African Americans in the 50s and 60s, it wasn't a realistic dream. However, Cole says he is a living testimony that by trusting God, anything is possible.

"We (Cole and his six sisters) grew up in the country, we picked cotton, and we were farmers," Cole said. "I was raised by my grandparents. Farming is what we did. During that time, it was a time when black folks didn't generally go to law school. I can testify that God has a way of blessing you, protecting you, and putting you where He wants you to be."

Cole said, seeing attorneys on television is what inspired him to want to become an attorney.

"I had no idea that it could actually come true, given our circumstances," Cole said, before explaining that while attending Rust College in the 1960s, the school had an exchange program with the University of Iowa, where he eventually came in contact with an attorney who needed work done, yard work is what Cole describes it as. Later, Cole found out about a program called the Council on Legal Education (CLEO), which was held at the University of Iowa. The purpose of the CLEO Program was (and still is) to give African Americans and minorities an opportunity to show that they could do legal work.

"The big problem was and still is that many African Americans score lower on the LSAT, the test that's used for admission to law school," Cole said. "This was a program for six weeks that gave African Americans an opportunity to show that they could do legal work. During the program, there were law schools recruiting African Americans to attend their law school. I fully intended to attend the University of Iowa Law School. I applied to the law school, and I was admitted, but I was not given any financial aid."

> *Given my family's situation, I, nor my*
> *grandparents had money to pay to go to law*
> *school or any of the expenses...*

Cole went on to note that he also applied to a few other law schools, but by the end of that summer in Iowa, he figured that there was no way for him to attend law school.

"I went back home from Iowa that summer not knowing what my next step would be," Cole recalled.

> *But then I got a letter in the mail from Drake*
> *University in Iowa, saying that I had*
> *been admitted, as well as I had been*
> *given a full scholarship...*

That was approximately a week and a half before school started in August 1969. The letter outlined instructions on when and how to report to the law school. But there was still a big problem. The letter stated that the school didn't have a dorm room for him to stay. In addition to that, Cole didn't have any money to travel from Mississippi to Iowa.

"The only thing that my grandfather was able to give me was $100," Cole said. "I had to decide if I was going to just stay in Mississippi, where I knew the outcome, that I would be a farmer or travel the unknown road and go to Iowa without having anywhere to stay. All I knew is that I wanted to be an attorney."

I decided to step out on faith to attend law school with $100 in my pocket and my clothes packed in a suitcase. No arrangements had been made for rooming, or a place for me to sleep at night...

Cole arrived at Drake University in Des Moines, Iowa and ended up in the Deans Office with his suitcase and no place to go. As a result of Cole's faith, the dean and the law school's staff helped arrange a place for him to stay for that night in temporary housing, and a few more nights after that, until they eventually found a permanent place for him to stay.

I really can't tell you how I made it on that $100, but I made it. I will just say that it was God's grace that he arranged and put people in my path who blessed me and showed favor toward me...

Cole noted that one person, in particular, who he believes God placed in his life for following his dream on faith, was an upper-class law student, who was married at the time with one child.

"They had a basement, and he allowed me to stay in his basement, so that was my first year in law school," Cole said. "After my first year, my financial situation wasn't much better, but still God provided a place for me to stay throughout the three years I was there and made it through law school. It was just God's provision, God making a way for me, for my dreams to be realized."

As for his academic struggles and adjustments to law school, Cole reflected on his first day of law school when one of his professors gave an assignment to brief five cases for the next day of class.

"I had no idea what he meant by briefing a case or how you go about briefing a case," Cole said. "There were other law students there whose dads had their own law firms, and they had been working in the law firms probably since before they were in high school and they knew all about that. I was in the class with people like that who pretty much knew the ins and outs of what was required, but I had no idea going in. But God had a way of providing, making a way, and seeing me through. By putting my faith in God and trusting Him despite my circumstances, I was able to realize my dream of becoming an attorney."

Cole passed the bar exam in 1973. Today, he serves as the Executive Director for North Mississippi Rural Legal Services in Oxford, Mississippi, providing legal assistance to individuals within a 39-county area. Cole has served the underprivileged as an attorney for more than 40 years in the Legal Service program.

WITH GOD, MY DREAM OF BECOMING A DOCTOR CAME TRUE

LORRAINE MCKINNEY
Houston, Texas

E ver since Lorraine McKinney was 12 years old, she had a dream of one day becoming a doctor, but along the way, she was told by many people whom she respected that becoming a doctor was something she could not accomplish. It would take a big leap of faith to go after her dream, and today she says it was only her trust in God leading and guiding her that allowed her to accomplish her dream.

"I went through school with being a doctor on my mind, even in college," McKinney recalled. "I was pre-med at Prairie View University. I had to tell my professors that, yes, I want to be a doctor. It was a known fact."

However, in 1992, her senior year at Prairie View University, McKinney says she had to ask professors for recommendation letters for her medical school application.

"I had one professor in particular who told me that I wouldn't make it in medical school and she refused to write a recommendation letter for me," McKinney said, before adding, "So I went and found another professor who believed in me, and he wrote the letter."

After approximately a year of applying to medical schools, McKinney was accepted into New York College Podiatric Medicine in 1993.

"I'm from Houston, Texas, and I was the first in my family to do anything like that, to go away to school," McKinney revealed.

All this time, I was just praying and asking God to open doors...

"To show me the way that He wanted me to go, because I felt like my calling was to be a doctor but I didn't know for sure what His will was, but I knew for me personally that I wanted to be a doctor," McKinney said.

McKinney went on to note that her freshman year in medical school was a tough year academically, having to adjust to the rigors of a medical school program. In fact, during the summer of 1994, McKinney said her academic performance came to a point to where she knew that if she did not make substantial improvements with her grades that she would not be allowed to continue in the program.

So I prayed like I had never prayed before...

"The coursework was 10 times more challenging than college," McKinney said. "I knew that God didn't bring me that far to leave me. I asked God in a way that I had never asked before to give me direction and to help me through this time, and if this is really what He wanted for me, to show me how to get through it, and show me how to get to the next level with my studies, to progress on to finish medical school."

McKinney noted that it was during this time of adversity in which the only thing she could do is put her faith and trust in God.

"I just remember recommitting myself to God again and leaning on Him in ways that I had never leaned on Him before," McKinney stressed. "It was like He opened a lot of different doors in ways that I can't even explain, but it was during this time, between my freshman and sophomore year in medical school that God showed me that this is what He wanted me to be and I just asked Him to use me as His instrument, his vessel, to be able to do the work that He has for me to do. He did that. It was just amazing. My testimony is that regardless of your circumstances, regardless of who supports you or doesn't support you, when you put your faith in God, all things are possible. I'm a living witness to it."

McKinney graduated from New York College Podiatric Medicine in 1998 before doing a residency in Richmond, Virginia. Beginning in 1999, McKinney served in private practice, nursing homes, assisted living facilities, and clinics in Central Virginia before returning to Texas in 2007 to address the foot care needs of those in the Greater Houston area. Dr. McKinney's practice focuses on preventing lower extremity amputations in diabetics through proactive foot care. Her website is *www.footandsole.com.*

CHAPTER 4
HEALTH

I WAS BLIND, BUT NOW I SEE

MICHAEL CHAMBERS
Monroe, Louisiana

L osing eyesight is something that Michael Chambers never thought would happen to him, but he says it was blindness that enlightened and strengthened his faith in Christ.

"In the summer of 2014, I started to see floaters in my eyes," Chambers recalled. "One Sunday, the floaters just started flying all around in my eyes like I had never seen before. By Monday morning, my retina had detached. I called my ophthalmologist, but he was in surgery, so I was recommended to another ophthalmologist. I was able to see her, the ophthalmologist, the same day. When she looked at my eye, she said my retina had detached, and that I needed to go to a retina eye specialist immediately. I was in downtown Houston when I got the news. My wife and sons were at work, so I had to drive myself roughly 20 miles, blind in one eye while my retina was about to detach in my other eye."

After being observed by the retina eye specialist, Chambers was told that he needed to have emergency surgery the next day.

"The next day I had surgery," Chambers said. "They were able to do laser surgery in my left eye and close the holes before the retina detached. They put the other retina back on and put a gas bubble behind my eye."

Surgery utilizing a gas bubble is commonly used to fix a retinal detachment.

I was in total darkness for the next
three to four months...

"I had to purchase a chair with a donut hole in it where I had to keep my head positioned face down around the clock," Chambers said. "I could not see. I could not watch any TV, and I could not hold my head up."

Chambers said that while he was without his vision, all he could do is put his trust and faith in the Lord.

"The Lord reassured me," Chambers said. "He told me that I was under His wings and that I didn't have to worry, because He was going to protect me and that no weapon formed against me will prosper. He told me that I was at His table and that He would provide for me. Then He told me that I was in His light, that He saw me, that He saw where I was, and that His grace was sufficient for me. He told me that His Word would be a lamp unto my feet and a light unto my pathway."

Chambers said he simply stood on God's promises while his faith was being tested.

"My sight was gone, but my other senses kicked in," Chambers said. "My hearing was better. I could hear Him more clearly. I spent months with the Lord just listening carefully. I had a closer walk with Him in that my relationship with Him grew stronger. I placed my faith in Him for the healing of my eyes."

My eye surgery was on September 9, 2014; by December, I began to see again...

"I'm fully healed, and total restoration has come," Chambers said. "The Lord gave me my sight back, and I am totally committed to what He has for me to do. I just thank Him for his grace and for His mercy."

"

I SURVIVED A DEATH DIAGNOSIS AFTER CONTRACTING HIV

TIFFANY QUINTON
Houston, Texas

n September 1995, Tiffany Quinton was diagnosed HIV positive and was told that she was going to die within a few weeks, but more than 22 years later, Quinton is still here, living, breathing, and enjoying life. She says it was only her faith and trust in God that allowed her to overcome what at the time seemed like a battle she could not win.

"I was 26 years old when I received the news that I had HIV," Quinton recalled.

But that was only the beginning. She had recently given birth to her son, Kyle, who was just nine months old when she received the news, changing her life forever.

It hit me like a ton of bricks. The only way I got through the actual shocking fear of being HIV positive is that I had to turn to God...

"I asked God for two things: To let me live and to let my baby be ok," Quinton recalled. "I trusted and believed that God would hear my prayer, and He did."

In fact, Quinton's son, Kyle, was born free of the HIV virus. Today, Kyle is a college student living a normal, healthy life.

"Some people saw and believed death was in my future, but God has used my life as a living testimony as to what God can do when you put your total trust in Him," Quinton stressed. "The hardest thing was to forgive. I had to forgive the guy that infected me because he didn't tell me that he was HIV positive. That was not an easy thing or an easy task."

But with God, everything is possible, so that's how I made it...

Quinton's days today are filled with workshops and public speaking engagements to bring awareness and prevention of HIV.

"I try to live as God wants me to live now by educating others about it," she said. "Life does not go the way you plan it. Life goes the way God plans it. HIV, cancer, anything is almost like a mind game. You have to have faith. Your faith has to live strong in Jesus. Through faith, you can get through anything. I did."

"

I SURVIVED A LIVER & KIDNEY TRANSPLANT

SHIRLEY ABRAHAM
Houston, Texas

I n need of a liver and kidney transplant, the family of Shirley Abraham was told by doctors that she only had two hours to live. That was more than seven years ago, and Abraham says it's only because of her faith in God that she is alive and well today.

"I had a liver and kidney transplant on April 26 (2010)," Abraham said. "I actually flat-lined on that day, that Monday morning, but the Lord wasn't ready for me yet. He spared my life for a purpose, and that purpose is to work with children at my church. Children are my pride and joy, besides God being in my life. I went to surgery for three days, the 26th, 27th, and the 28ᵗʰ of April."

Within those three days, I had 25 hours of surgery...

"I could only put my faith in God," Abraham said. "My story is that I am a believer. I know that God had his hands on me when He brought me through surgery. I love the Lord and my favorite song is, 'I love the Lord, He heard my cry, and He pitted my grown.' And as long as I live, I will serve Him. God is great to me. He has been my joy, and right now, my heart is heavy because I thank him for every morning that He allows me to see another day. And I thank Him for allowing me to see 70 years of life. He said in his Word that He would give us three scores and 10, and I saw my three scores and 10, which was Thanksgiving Day of 2015. I thank God for every year that I've been here on this earth.

I know that I am a miracle, that God had His hands upon me. I needed a liver and kidney transplant. I placed my faith in

Christ when it looked like I wasn't going to make it, but I'm still here. I'm a testimony that no matter what you're going through or what you're facing if you place your faith and trust in Him, He can work it out for you."

"I BEAT CANCER

BEN DUNCAN
Louisville, Kentucky

F or Ben Duncan, trusting in God has always been at the forefront of his mind, but when cancer showed up in his life, not once, not twice, but three times, his faith in God went to a whole new level.

In 1999, Duncan's wife was diagnosed with colon cancer shortly after she retired.

"She gave it a good fight, but she succumb to the effects of cancer two days before Christmas on December 23, 2000," said Duncan.

That was his first bout with cancer. Shortly afterward, he met and married his second wife, who was later diagnosed with breast cancer.

"I was saying, God, you've taken me through one trial with cancer, now you're taking me through another one," Duncan recalled. "I kept saying that I know it's to strengthen me, but I also asked the Lord, what are you trying to tell me? He told me that I was there to provide her with the support she needed."

With his devotion to prayer, faith, and support, Duncan's wife, Iola, beat cancer and is alive and well today. But his battle with cancer wasn't over. In 2012, he was diagnosed with cancer, prostate cancer.

"I went through 46 doses of radiation and chemotherapy," Duncan said, before adding, "I know that through prayer and being obedient to God that it was Him who kept me and made me stronger."

Duncan stressed that it was only his faith in God that got him through all three of his bouts with cancer, the health condition that has taken the lives of so many people around the world. He went on to note that although his first wife died from cancer, his second wife beat it, and he himself beat cancer that something was gained in each experience with cancer. That something, according to Duncan, is that God's will was done in each bout with cancer.

> ### *By my count, cancer did not win one time; God is 3-0...*

Today, Duncan's devotion to God has increased as a result of the trials and tribulations he has experienced with cancer.

"I just love working for the Lord, and I just hope that what I've said will help somebody along the way," Duncan said. "God is good, and through faith in Him, He will heal you. He healed me."

"

I SURVIVED AN ANEURYSM

GEORGETTE PAYNE
Houston, Texas

eorgette Payne believes that faith is one of the most important aspects of life for all Christians. But when she found herself having to decide whether to have surgery to heal a thoracic aortic aneurysm that was discovered behind her left eye, a decision that could leave her blind for life, she says that placing her faith in Christ for guidance was the best thing she could have ever done.

"My other option was not to have surgery and risk the possibility of the aneurysm growing and rupturing at any given time, possibly causing my death," Payne said.

Payne's medical issue all started on a Wednesday night in March 2014. Payne was helping with her church's Wednesday night Bible study, something in which she has routinely done each Wednesday night for several years. But on this particular night, Payne started to experience a migraine-like pain in her head.

"I went home that night, and the next day, I headed to work as I normally did," Payne recalled. "While I was at work, I felt an excruciating pain in my head. I called and told my husband that I needed to go to the emergency room."

Once there, the hospital staff, Payne said, ran a CAT scan. Fully expecting the result of the CAT scan to be that she simply needed medicine to relieve her headache. Payne, however, was told that she needed an MRI.

"The MRI showed that I didn't have a migraine, but that I had a left thoracic aortic aneurysm," Payne said. "It threw me into shock because all I heard was aneurysm."

The aneurysm was located behind her left eye. However, the actual pain she was experiencing was on the right side of her head.

"We couldn't figure out how that could be," Payne said. "The doctor said my case was classified as an incidental finding, meaning what was discovered was not what I came into the hospital for. They admitted me the same day, and I stayed in the hospital for three days. Several neurosurgeons came to visit me. They were giving me options and telling me the size of the aneurysm."

Ultimately, I was given a choice: to leave the aneurysm alone, which meant that I would be taking a chance that it could grow on its own, rupture and I possibly die, or have the surgery and lose my sight in that eye...

"The doctor told me that if I go in and have the surgery, it's a great chance that I would not see out of that eye again," Payne said. "I really broke down after that, because it was like, if I have the surgery, I'm not going to be able to see."

Payne, however, decided to seek a second opinion from other neurosurgeons.

"The doctors did not want to do the surgery, not because of the size of the aneurysm, but because of its location," Payne said.

My husband and I prayed about it. We went back to the doctor and informed the doctor that we were going to step out on faith and have the surgery...

"He (the doctor) drew it out with a pen and paper and showed me the size of the aneurysm and told me again that I may not be able to see out of my eye again if I have this surgery," Payne said. "But since we prayed about it, we decided to place our faith in God. We went ahead with the surgery, although we knew the risks."

The surgery took several hours. The end result: the surgery was a complete success.

"The weirdest thing is that after the surgery, not only could I see, I was on Facebook in ICU the same day from the surgery," Payne said. "I had not one side effect. No dizziness, nothing."

I consider myself blessed; it was defiantly a test of my faith...

"I'm glad that my husband and I made the decision to have the surgery, because if we didn't make the decision to have the surgery, the aneurysm could have kept growing, and the doctor told me that if the person doesn't have the surgery and it keeps growing, at any given time it could rupture, usually causing death," Payne said. "The doctor told me that the time between life and death with an aneurysm is literally minutes. Once it ruptures, if you don't get straight to where you need to be, the doctor says it's a slim chance you'll make it to the ER alive. In my case, I stepped out on faith, and I was able to go back to work and live my life as usual just a few weeks after my surgery. I thank God. He gets all the glory."

I SURVIVED WALKING PNEUMONIA

MELVIN DEBERRY
Holly Springs, Mississippi

Melvin Deberry has lived most of his life virtually free of serious illness, but when an unexpected case of walking pneumonia left him hospitalized, he says it was only his faith in God and the prayers of a community of Christian believers that made it possible for him to be alive and well today.

"The last weekend in June 2016, I had to go to the hospital," Deberry recalled. "I had fluid that built up on my lungs. I couldn't breathe, so they had to put a tube in my side to pump the fluid. I stayed in the hospital, Methodist Hospital in Germantown, Tennessee. I was in critical condition. I stayed in intensive care for three days."

At one point they thought I wasn't going to make it...

Walking pneumonia, also known as bacterial pneumonia, consists of germs that enter the lungs, which can overpower the immune system and invade nearby lung tissues, which are very delicate. Once infected, the lungs' air sacs inflame and fill up with fluid and pus, which causes coughing, fever, chills, and breathing problems, symptoms in which Deberry endured.

Deberry said while he was on his sickbed, all he could do is place his faith and trust in God's hands to allow him to continue living. He said God honored his faith.

"I got out of the hospital on the 13th day of July," Deberry said, before adding, "I had to have surgery to walk around. Physically, I was weak, but I got over that, and today, I feel pretty good. The spirit side is that God brought me through. I know that as people, we get down sometimes, but when you pray and have faith in Him, it seems like things just work out for you. You get stronger."

Deberry said his health ordeal showed him the power of having a community of believers (his church, friends, and family) praying for the same thing: his life.

"It just makes you feel good when you have people praying for you," Deberry said. "I'm thankful that God kept me a little while longer."

"

I WAS DIAGNOSED WITH
LYMPHOMA, BUT THROUGH
FAITH IN CHRIST, NOW
I'M HEALED

YOLANDA SAM
Houston, Texas

When Yolanda Sam was diagnosed with lymphoma, a type of blood cancer, in February 2014, it was the last thing that she thought she would hear. She was in shock, scared, and worried about what her diagnoses meant for her children and husband, but she says by placing her faith in Jesus Christ, her body was healed and is now in remission.

"I'm a living testimony to others that if He healed me, He can heal them too," Sam said, before admitting that when she was diagnosed, "the one thing that I was very concerned about is not knowing the outcome."

Not knowing the outcome of her condition, she says, is when her faith in God played a major role in her healing.

I knew that I was going to have to go through chemo...

"When I was first diagnosed, the doctors said that it was too early for me to go through chemo, so I was on the wait-and-see list to see if it would spread or get bad enough to where I would need chemo," Sam said. "I was afraid for my children. I kept thinking to myself, what would happen to them? I kept saying; I can't go anywhere because I have to take care of my children, and my husband still needed me. We needed each other."

After approximately a year and a half of being in the wait-and-see category, Sam said she started feeling the side effects of cancer.

"The doctors told me that it was time for chemo and I just didn't want to accept that," Sam said.

But I also knew that by His stripes, I am healed…

"This was something that was totally out of my control, so I couldn't do anything but put my faith in God and trust that He would heal me," Sam recalled. "As the chemo was going through my body, I had to believe that I was healed. I had to remember that God created everything. He created the doctors, nurses, and that all of these people had gifts, and I had to know that because He created everything, the medicine He created through man, would do what it was supposed to do."

Through faith and trust in God, Sam said the medicine worked.

"In February 2017, I went into remission," Sam said, before adding, "If He did it for me, He can do it for you too."

"

I'M FREE OF THROAT CANCER

CATHERINE TODD
Byhalia, Mississippi

A t 1 p.m. each Friday, Catherine Todd can be heard on WKRA 92.7 FM radio station giving an encouraging message of the Gospel and prayer to thousands of people across the Mid-South region. But she says had it not been for her faith in God when she was diagnosed with thyroid cancer in 2003, none of it would be possible today.

Thyroid cancer, according to WebMD, is an uncommon type of cancer in which medical researchers and experts are not sure what causes it. However, Todd said her life instantly changed when doctors called and notified her that she had cancer.

"It was very, very frightening," Todd recalled, before adding, "They told me that there was a chance that I wasn't going to ever be able to talk again, that I was going to lose my voice."

Todd went on to explain that in July 2003, she started feeling a lingering tingle in her throat, similar to having a scratchy voice during a regular cold. She, however, decided to check with her doctor, who then noticed something unusual around her neck. Several x-rays were done, resulting in Todd's doctor recommending that she have thyroid surgery. Her surgery was performed on August 23, 2003.

"It was supposed to be a four-hour surgery, but it turned out to be an eight-hour surgery," Todd said.

During surgery, they found a thyroid tumor the size of a golf ball; then they found a blood clot, the blood clot was trapped in my brain...

"I had a lot of complications where they had to put the breathing tube in me, it was very serious," said Todd, who remained in the hospital for six days due to the complications related to the surgery. "My face had swollen to the size of two heads, but through faith and prayer, I can say that by the grace of God, He brought me through. I was very frightened, but I can say that everything came out well."

Todd went on to stress that she is sharing her story to encourage others who have been diagnosed with any form of cancer, that by faith in Christ and placing their lives in God's hands, they can be healed the same way that she was.

"The doctor said that many people don't make it with thyroid cancer because it can spread so rapidly," Todd said. "I prayed to God. I trusted Him. I had faith in Him. I believed in Him. I believed His word that He is a healer. I underwent only one treatment of chemotherapy, and by the grace of God, I have been cancer-free for more than 14 years," Todd said.

Today, Todd can be heard on the radio at 1 p.m. central standard time each Friday via live streaming at *thechange927.com.*

"

I WAS TOLD I ONLY HAD 24 HOURS TO LIVE

JUDITH SCARBOROUGH
Hampton, Georgia

Judith Scarborough is not supposed to be alive today. Death, according to doctors, was just a few hours away for her, but she says her faith in God to do the miraculous, is what kept her alive nearly 20 years ago.

"On December 18, 1998, I became very ill with a flesh-eating virus, which at that time, doctors didn't know what it was, so they couldn't diagnose what was wrong with me," Scarborough recalled. "I was told that in the next 24 hours, I would not be alive."

At that moment, Scarborough, who is not sure how she contracted the mysterious flesh-eating disease she had, said she did the only thing that she could do: pray to God and have faith that He would deliver her.

"I saw a sign from God that told me that He would never leave me, nor forsake me," Scarborough said, before adding, "I could see the still water in the skies that were blue and all I could remember that evening was reciting Psalms 23."

It was eating my insides, I lost four fingers, and I lost the body mass in my legs...

"I wasn't able to walk, and I'm permanently disabled," Scarborough said, before adding that she leaned on God to intercede and save her life.

"I had faith," she said. "Each day, God would give me a sign, and each day for over 18 months, He gave me a sign to let me know that He would never leave me, nor forsake me. I believe there is a true God in heaven that will never leave you, nor forsake you. I will tell anybody to lean on God because He is there for you and

He will never leave you, nor forsake you. They told my husband to prepare for me to be buried because I only had 24 hours at most to live, but God proved them wrong. After 24 hours had passed, I was still alive, and I'm still alive today, thanks to my faith in Him."

GOD KEPT ME WHEN A SIMPLE PROCEDURE SUDDENLY BECAME A MAJOR PROBLEM

CAMILLA BLOSSOM
Salt Lake City, Utah

For Camilla Blossom, having faith in God is much more than saying it out loud. Having faith in God is being able to trust Him even when you can't speak, stand, sit, or move a single limb on your body.

That's exactly what she had to do after she was given too much anesthesia during a medical procedure in January 2003.

"I was not able to move or feel anything," said Blossom. "I could hear conversations of the medical staff who were there in the room with me, but I could not talk. I could tell that something was not right, so I began to pray silently and asked the Lord to take care of me."

Blossom explained that the reason she was undergoing anesthesia to begin with was due to a slip and fall accident that happened several months before. She was experiencing severe sciatic nerve pain as a result of the fall.

"Approximately two months after the fall, I began to feel unbearable pain from sciatica," Blossom explained.

Sciatica is a condition associated with constant pain in a person's legs and buttocks and is often hard to walk, sit, or stand.

"My doctor recommended that I do physical therapy," Blossom recalled, before adding, "Having completed physical therapy, I was still experiencing pain. I was then referred to have an epidural to help alleviate the pain. I went ahead and set up the epidural appointment, an appointment that should not have lasted more than one hour and 30 minutes, but I was there all day because something happened."

I was paralyzed....

It was discovered that Blossom was given too much anesthesia during the procedure and as a result, was in a paralyzed state.

"The staff repeatedly asked if I could feel anything," said Blossom. "I could not feel anything. They kept checking on me every 15 to 30 minutes or so until I could feel a touch. I could hear the thud of the touch, but I could not feel it. I continued to pray and ask the Lord to help me."

> *I was really scared because I could hear them speaking, I couldn't open my mouth, but my eyes were open...*

"The staff decided to try to get me up," Blossom said. "It was all dead weight. I had to drag one foot in front of the other. All I could do is place my faith in Christ to help me at this point. Slowly but surely the life began to come back into my leg. I know that He allowed everything and everybody to be there for a purpose. I thank Him for allowing me to be able to walk out of that building, and I know it was due to faith and His grace and His mercy on me."

WITH GOD, I BEAT BREAST CANCER

IOLA DUNCAN
Houston, Texas

According to statistics from BreastCancer.org, 1 in 8 U.S. women will develop invasive breast cancer over the course of her lifetime. In addition, more than 40,000 women in the United States are expected to die each year from breast cancer. And when Iola Duncan was diagnosed with breast cancer in 2005, she was well aware of the statistics and the high possibility of death, but she says it was her faith in Christ that allowed her to beat it.

"I believe my diagnosis of breast cancer made me stronger because I believe that God would not give you more than you can bear, so it's a true testimony for me," said Duncan, who became a believer in Christ and baptized at the age of 12.

As for her diagnosis, Duncan was attending a conference in San Antonio in 2005 when she noticed a lump.

"I went to get it checked, and I was diagnosed with breast cancer," Duncan recalled. "At the time, I was more concerned about my family. I have three sisters who have health issues. I remember telling the doctors to give me a lighter dose of chemo because, throughout my life, I was pretty healthy. My doctor said no since you're so healthy, you can get the strongest dose because your body can take it and that will knock it right out."

Duncan went on to compare her battle and challenges with cancer to the challenges all humans face in life.

"Christ allows us to go through challenges in life, but He allows those challenges because He knows that we can face those challenges," she said, before adding, "Through faith, we can fight, using His Word. And we know that because we're stronger, we're going to come up against more obstacles."

Duncan, a wife, a mother of three sons, a grandmother with six brothers and three sisters, said just as it was with her cancer diagnosis, God has always put her in a place where she could help others.

"I'm grateful, and I'm humbled by it," Duncan said. "A lot of times, the weight of the world seems like it's on you, but we can always lean on God when the challenges are very strong. I am a living witness to everyone that regardless of what you go through when you put your trust and faith in Christ, He can bring you out."

THE DOCTORS SAID IT WAS OVER, BUT I'M STILL HERE

CHRISTOPHER SUTTON

When Christopher Sutton's mother passed away on July 1, 2015, from having an abscess on her body, it was one of the hardest things in his life to accept. However, six months later, he found himself fighting for his life with the same condition, but he credits his faith in Christ for having the strength to pull through it.

"I was fighting for my life," Sutton recalled. "In the book of Job, he said I knew about God, but now I know Him for myself. When I was younger I used to hear the old preachers saying that God is a healer, God is a way maker, and growing up in the church I would say that's all good, but now I can say that I know Him for myself to be a healer."

It was February 2016, when Sutton, a two-time world champion, who is listed in the state, national, and world record books for the single ply-bench press of 867 pounds, discovered an abscess on his thigh.

"It started off small, and it grew big," Sutton said of the abscess, which according to the Mayo Clinic, is a pocket of painful puss on the body that carries bacterial infection.

"It got so big that I tried home remedies to keep from going to the hospital," Sutton said. "It didn't work. It just got bigger and bigger."

My whole body just shut down...

"It was on a Friday, I was driving, but I don't even know how I made it home," Sutton explained. "My wife rushed me to the hospital. When we got to the hospital, my chest was hurting; everything was collapsing. They rushed me back, and the abscess on my right thigh ruptured inside my body, and essentially, my whole body had an infection. Everything was just falling apart. I was fighting for my life. I was trying to breathe, and my life just started flashing right before my eyes."

Reflecting on the fact that his mother went into the hospital for an abscess just a few months earlier, and died from the complications of her conditions, Sutton, also the pastor of Open Hands Bible Fellowship Church in Houston, said he knew he needed help from whence his help comes from: God.

"I held my mother's hand as I watched her go on to glory," Sutton said, before adding, "so now I have an abscess on the same spot, so I'm fearful for my life. The doctors said it was all over for me. The medicine didn't work, but I just kept praying and praying. People were praying for me because I was really sedated for a whole week. A week later, I began to come to and realize who I was."

But in the midst of fighting for his life, Sutton said, he found himself in a position to witness the Gospel of Christ while in the hospital.

"There was a nurse there that didn't know Jesus, and I ended up witnessing to her," Sutton said, noting that shortly after sharing the Gospel of Jesus Christ with the nurse, he was released from the hospital.

"They sent me home with a pinch in my right arm that led from my bicep, all the way to my heart, so for three weeks to a month, I had to continuously inject medicine into my body because the oral medication wasn't strong enough," Sutton said. "That was an ordeal all by itself, but when I look back at it, I said, God, did you have me going to the hospital for that lady, for me to minister to her? I just begin to rejoice, saying God keep using me however you can. I was there ministering to that lady about the goodness of Jesus, and how wonderful and powerful my God is. She was able to see how powerful my God is and how, by my faith in Jesus Christ, I was healed."

Sutton stressed that this event in his life is a testimony to how faith in Christ can not only save your own life but also someone else's eternal life by being in a position to be a witness and vessel of the power of God.

"It taught me a lesson that if you say you want to be used by God, sometimes God will allow you to be in a bad situation to reach somebody because they need to be able to hear the Gospel," Sutton said. "And if it took for me to get into the hospital to reach that nurse, it was all worth it, fighting for my life, and going through all of that because I recognize how wonderful and awesome my God is."

I SURVIVED AN AMNIOTIC FLUID EMBOLISM

FANNIE EDDY

F annie Eddy has always wanted to be married with children, but when an unexpected medical emergency happened while she was giving birth to her son, she says, it was only the power of God that allowed her to survive and live to talk about it today.

"It was December 19, 1990, when my son was born," Eddy said. "But when I went into the hospital that day to give birth via C-section, it was discovered that I had an amniotic fluid embolism, a condition that's pretty rare and when women do have it, my doctors told me that women usually don't survive. At that time in 1990, my doctor told me that only one in 250,000 women would survive an amniotic fluid embolism. This was a test of my faith."

According to the Mayo Clinic, an amniotic fluid embolism is a rare but serious condition that occurs when amniotic fluid—the fluid that surrounds a baby in the uterus during pregnancy—or fetal material, such as fetal cells, enters the mother's bloodstream. It's estimated, according to the Mayo Clinic's statistics in 2017, that there are between one and twelve cases of amniotic fluid embolism for every 100,000 deliveries.

My medical charts indicated that I basically died on the operating table...

"My body, due to my condition (amniotic fluid embolism), started pushing fluid out, and when they saw my body was rejecting, the only way to stop my body from hemorrhaging was to have a hysterectomy, immediately," Eddy recalled, before adding, "They were saving my life by removing my uterus to stop me from bleeding out."

But there was another big problem...

"I have O Negative blood," Eddy said of her blood type, which according to the America Red Cross, only 7 percent of the population has. "I can give blood, and most everyone can accept O Negative blood, but I can't accept any other kind of blood. I have to have O Negative blood."

Eddy, taking her story back to before her surgery, recalled that something unusual happened prior to her giving birth to her son, something in which she believes was an act of God saving her life through the mouth of her then, three-year-old daughter.

"Before I went into the hospital that day, my daughter started saying that she didn't want me to go to the hospital because she didn't want me to die," Eddy said. "She was really loud and frantic about it. After everything was said and done, the doctor told me that since my daughter was so adamant about it, he, without telling me, ordered O Negative blood just in case something happened."

As a result, the right type of blood was on hand, and her son was born without any complications.

Eddy, whose son is now 26 years old and in college studying to be an engineer, said her faith was tested during this event. She went on to note that looking back on what happened; she can testify that it was only her faith in God that brought her out of a situation in which most women don't survive.

"I think that God wanted to show me that He loves me intimately, so that I could know it for myself, and not because somebody else told me He loves me," Eddy said. "He wanted me to know that He truly loves me and that He wasn't going to let anything happen to me. You have to trust and believe that He will bring you out of whatever situation you're in, and because of my experience, when my faith is tested today, now I don't have any fear because I can think back and remember what He has already done for me. I only hope that telling my story and sharing what God has done for me, helps someone, somewhere, know that God is real."

CHAPTER 5
STRESS & WORRY

"

I WORRY NO MORE

KARL LAVINE
New Iberia, Louisiana

ccording to statistics, more than 40 million people suffer from worrying and anxiety and has proven to be a vehicle that leads to major illnesses, even death. Worrying is something Karl Lavine says was a huge part of his life until he gave everything over to his Lord and Savior, Jesus Christ.

"It was a big level of faith for me to put everything in the hands of God," Lavine said. "Specifically, I went through a divorce in 1985, and in that divorce, I had a problem with worrying, worrying about money, worrying about divorce, worrying about my kids, and really worrying about my future."

Like many people across the world, Lavine says, worrying was a constant in his life, but noted that he finally found solace after hearing a sermon preached from Matthew 6:25-34.

"The sermon was about not worrying," Lavine recalled. "The preacher listed the four Ps. Live on the promise. Live in the present. Pray continuously. Be patient. In this passage of scripture, Jesus said, don't worry about anything. Don't worry about the lilies in the field because they are here today and gone tomorrow. Don't worry about what's going to happen. Matthew 6:33 says, 'Seek ye first the Kingdom of God and His righteousness, and He shall provide all of these things to you. Not all of what you want, but all of what you need. You have to live for today and today alone because tomorrow is not promised. The whole idea is that you have to live for today. You can't worry about what's going to happen tomorrow. You can't go back and recapture yesterday, so you have to live for today.'"

Lavine stressed that over the years, he has learned that when we depend on God for everything that we have, He is true to His

Word that He's going to take care of every need that we have, so there is no need to worry.

In addition, Lavine noted that believers have to be in constant communication with God and by being in constant communication with God, He will direct us where ever we need to go if we give Him total control of where we are and whose we are.

"God has a specific time for us," Lavine testified, before adding, "And in that specific time He takes care of every aspect of our blessings. And over the years, this has resonated in my mind to give God the glory and to be patient, because He's going to take care of every need."

Lavine's testimony is that everything that he used to worry about during his divorce in 1985 was already taken care of.

I remarried. I have been married for 23 years, and I have a great relationship with my nine children, 28 grandchildren, and three great-grandchildren...

"God has continuously blessed me, though that didn't stop problems from coming my way, but when you can go back to the Word that says, don't worry, it is something that you can stand on because it is in His written Word," Lavine said. "I made it through, and I can testify that by stepping out on faith to not worry about things that are presented to me in this life, I worry no more because my faith and trust are in Christ."

"

I FELT LIKE GIVING UP,
BUT GOD HAD OTHER PLANS

DONIEL WATTS
Houston, Texas

Regardless of how bad things get, whether it's a loss of a job, health issues, money issues, relationship issues, or anything else in between, Doniel Watts says she is proof that even when you're at the lowest point in your life, putting your faith in God is the best decision anyone can make.

"In December 2004, I got really, really sick," said Watts. "I was admitted to Methodist Hospital in Sugar Land, Texas. All I can remember is drifting in and out because I was on so many different pain medicines while I was in ICU. I actually thought I was in hell."

> ### *I remember the doctor telling my husband at the time that they didn't think I was going to make it...*

Watts was in a coma-like state.

"I felt like giving up, things were bad in my life," Watts said. "I hadn't worked in a year. I lost my car; I had problems in my marriage because I could not do the things I was financially able to when I was working. After I heard that I wasn't going to make it, all I remember is closing my eyes."

Watts said she remembers praying to God and telling God that she was sorry for wanting to give up on her life due to her circumstances.

"I promised God that I was going to try harder, and I tried my best to wake up from whatever I was in," Watts stressed. "After praying and praying and asking God to help me, I finally woke up and I got better. I knew from then on that there is a God, and that's when I started to turn everything over to Him, emulating Him in every aspect of my life. I put my faith and trust in God, and I'm a living witness that when you do that, He can turn any situation around. It's the best decision anyone can make."

Today, Watts is gainfully employed as a teacher in the Houston Independent School District. God has replaced the vehicle she lost, and her family is together.

CHAPTER 6
FINANCES

MY HUSBAND & I LOST NEARLY EVERYTHING, BUT OUR FAITH IN CHRIST PULLED US THROUGH

ROSALIND LEE
Sugar Land, Texas

Being in love with Jesus Christ is something that Rosalind Lee has kept near and dear to her heart, but it wasn't until she and her husband, Jonathan lost nearly everything that they owned that she learned to totally trust and have true faith in Him.

"My faith and my husband's faith was truly tested when we came to financial ruin," said Lee. "We had a very, very lucrative business for many years. That business afforded us the opportunity to go into any store, the high retail stores like Neiman Marcus, Bergdorf Goodman, and more. If we desired it, we got it. It (the business' success) afforded us vacations to Bermuda, Hawaii, we just lived a good, solid financial life, but we weren't selfish with our finances. We gave lavishly. We gave to our church. We gave to the needs of our community and to the surrounding schools, so we weren't selfish."

The Lee's owned a private ambulance service with a wide variety of contracts, contracts with dollar amounts that gave them the opportunity to purchase their dream home.

"We actually sat down with an architect and planned our home, what rooms we would have, what the rooms would look like, where the rooms would go, where the bathrooms would go," Lee explained. "We built our home from the ground up. It was located behind a gated wall, on the lake. We just knew that this would be our lasting spot, and we were looking forward to retirement. The Lord allowed us to live in that home for 12 years. We had a swimming pool in the backyard, the grandchildren would come over and just have a ball, and friends would come over too. It was beautiful."

But in 2006, our faith was tested, it brought us to our knees, and it shook our faith in God...

Through a series of events, it was discovered that over a million dollars had been embezzled from their business.

"We lost our business as a result of that," Lee revealed, before adding, "I fell into a state of depression."

Lee said at one point; she started drinking wine often just to be able to go to sleep.

"But God being who He is, He didn't allow me to stay that way, though," Lee said. "God said enough is enough, Rosalind, raise up because your faith is being tested."

Lee noted that she equates the financial loss to the story of Job in the Bible, where the Lord permitted Satan to try His servant, Job. Job, described in the Bible as a wealthy, blameless, and upright man, lost all of his possessions: 7,000 sheep, 3,000 camels, 500 yokes of oxen, 500 female donkeys, and seven sons and three daughters. In the end, God blessed Job with twice as much as he had before his trials began.

"I believe God said the same thing concerning us: have you tried Jonathan and Rosalind Lee? And the Lord said you can try them, but you cannot touch their soul, which he (Satan) did not do," Lee stressed.

We lost our home of 12 years, and we had to move into a two-bedroom apartment...

"Even now several years later, we still have not fully recuperated from that, because it was so devastating," Lee said. "We pulled from our savings to try to save a home that God told us to let go. We pulled from our retirement funds because we didn't realize that it was God working through the midst of this."

Lee, however, said she and her husband were able to truly live out the true meaning of trusting the Lord and placing their faith in Christ.

"Our faith is strengthened and what we can do today is be an encourager for those younger people who are going in that same direction," Lee said. "I tell them to have a closer relationship with the Lord, so when He tells you it's time to move, front, back, left, or right, you will know clearly that He is speaking and that you line up with what He has for your life. You really will not know that you have faith until your faith is tested, and that's when you will know that without faith, it is impossible to please God (Hebrews 11:6)."

Lee said that she and her husband are living testimonies that when you place your faith in God in whatever you're going through, He will be there for you and in the end, just like Job, God will bless you.

"We're blessed," Lee said.

CHRIST STRENGTHENED ME & I MADE IT THROUGH

PATRICIA JOHNSON
Richmond, Texas

n 2011, Patricia Johnson found herself in a position in which she never thought she would be in: divorced and in over her head in debt, but she credits her faith in God for the reason she was able to make it through during a time in which she wasn't so sure she could.

"After my divorce, I was left with having to pay for a mortgage all on my own, a car note, caring for my daughter, who would be entering college soon, and other things to where I started to wonder if I needed to do something else professionally in order to pay for it all," said Johnson, a professional hairstylist in Sugar Land, Texas. "I got married for all of the wrong reasons."

The marriage only lasted nine months, and we were divorced...

"I really didn't know how I was going to pay for everything, so the only thing that I could do is ask for God to help me," Johnson recalled. "As Christians, we all talk about how we have to trust in Jesus, but it becomes real when you are put into circumstances where the only thing you can do is trust Him to help you."

I prayed a lot...

"I couldn't see my way out, but once I let go and simply went on faith that everything would work out, God was able to step in and do what He does," said Johnson. "By the grace of God, I made it through this. I went through a time that many people go through, financial things that many people don't think that they can get through, but I am a witness that by trusting Him and placing your total faith and belief in Him, He can make a way when you don't see that a way can be made."

Today, Johnson is a successful real estate agent and owner of Beautifully Made Hair Salon in Sugar Land, Texas. Her daughter is attending Prairie View A & M University.

" IT WAS LIKE GOD SENT TWO ANGELS TO RESTORE MY HEALTH & FINANCIAL TROUBLES

JOE WILSON
Chicago, Illinois

J oe Wilson, a United States Veteran, has always believed in taking life head-on and overcoming challenges, something he has successfully done most of his life, but he says a string of financial and health issues that showed up in his life in 2002 is something he could not fight on his own and that God is the only one who was able to save him.

Wilson, in 2002, was working as a contractor for Direct TV, where he was making $1,200 a day some days and on a slow day, making $400 a day.

"I was on top of the world," Wilson said. "I had money in the bank, I had two daughters in college at the time, so I bought both of them cars, and I bought myself a new truck, in addition to the house, I bought. Everything was just beautiful, financially speaking."

But in 2005, Wilson said he started having health problems, where several surgeries were needed to remove boils from his body.

"As a result of the surgeries, I couldn't get around, and I couldn't get any work, everything just shut down on me," Wilson said.

Things got so bad that my truck was repossessed, and in May 2006, I received a notice that my house was in the final stages of foreclosure...

"I really didn't know what to do or how to solve my problems," Wilson said. "I even applied for social security and veteran's connected disability in hopes of getting some financial relief, but I was denied for the veteran's disability. I was in a state of depression. Here I was, a person who has always helped others financially, and I was on the verge of not having anywhere to stay. I was really down, and I didn't want to be a burden to anyone. I had no income, so I didn't see a way out."

But then God stepped in…

"Right before my home was to be auctioned off, I got a call from Veteran's Affairs in St. Petersburg, Florida, in June 2006, and the guy on the phone told me that they were the guarantors of my mortgage and just like that, I was granted an extension until September. It was like an angel had swooped down to save me. The social security started to come in soon afterward, and I was able to get into bankruptcy protection."

But Wilson said his problems weren't over. Wilson started receiving calls for unpaid student loans.

"I thought I was fine after the bankruptcy, but bankruptcy doesn't wipe out the student loans, so it was like my financial problems came back and hit me again when I thought things were getting better," Wilson stressed."

In addition to that, on Aug. 12, 2008, his health problems returned. This time, he had to stay in the hospital for 90 days. However, it was during this time that it was discovered that he had been misdiagnosed since 1975 as having severe acne, a reason why his veteran's disability was denied. But after praying for God's help, Wilson said it was discovered that the condition he actually had, a condition in which his sweat glands would shut down, causing boils to form, was not acne, but a rare condition called hidradenitis suppurativa.

Hidradenitis suppurativa, which has no cure, according to WebMD, causes painful bumps under the skin near sweat glands, located under the arms, in the groin, and between the buttocks.

I was in severe pain, and God heard my prayer.…

"I had been getting misdiagnose for over 30 years, but God heard my prayer and sent another angel in the form of a doctor to find out what was really going on with my health," Wilson said. "My testimony is that as a result of this, I was able to get approved for 100 percent veteran's disability. With 100 percent veteran's disability, the $46,000 in student loans was wiped away. This was the hardest time in my life, but I can say that it was God who stepped in on my behalf. I am a witness that prayers through faith in God are answered. I went through a storm, and it was tough going through it, but now I have been properly diagnosed to get proper treatment, and my financial problems have been restored."

"

I WENT FROM NEARLY LOSING MY HOME TO SELLING IT FOR A PROFIT

KAM CHARLES
Converse, Texas

T he year 2010 was a very freighting time for Kam Charles. The mother of three children found herself in a state of depression after she and her husband of 18 years divorced, leaving her with a mortgage she couldn't afford on her own, a car note, and an assortment of other bills. But she says once she put her trust in God to make a way...He did.

"Prior to us getting divorced my ex-husband was the financial breadwinner," Charles said. "He paid all of the bills; he paid the mortgage, everything, except for my car note and cell phone bill. But after the divorce, I ended up having to take on the mortgage, because he gave me the house, and all of the other bills that came along with it."

My paycheck wasn't enough money to pay all of my bills; several times, I thought about letting the house go...

"My car was almost paid off at the time, but it was still a struggle because I didn't know where I would get the money to pay for everything every month," Charles recalled, before adding, "The only thing I could do was pray and stay faithful to God, and He made a way out of no way."

I received two raises and promotions on my job in one year, which was something that normally doesn't happen.....

"I was almost about to lose my house," Charles said. "The banks will work with you sometimes, but I was constantly on the phone with them trying to help me make arrangements so that I wouldn't lose it, because I needed a place for my kids to live. The banks put a couple of my house payments to the end of the loan, but they were still expecting the mortgage payment every month."

Charles, however, said that God rewarded her for her faith in Him to provide for her and her family when she wasn't fully able to.

"With the second promotion I received, I was able to receive bonuses based on my work," Charles explained. "With the promotion and bonuses, I was able to pay off my car. To this day, I still don't know how I did that. I still think about that, how God allowed me to pay off my car note."

I think about how He never let me miss a meal, my kids never missed a meal, and my kids didn't even know what I was going through, or how close I was to losing the house...

Charles said that by placing her faith in God, a divine door was opened for her to refinance her house, allowing her to keep the home, and in July 2016, she was able to sell her home for a profit.

"Things just started falling into place," Charles said. "I know that it was nobody but God because I couldn't have done it on my own at all."

"

GOD PROVIDED FOR MY FAMILY WHEN WE COULDN'T PROVIDE FOR OURSELVES

CLARENCE WOODS
Eldorado, Arkansas

Growing up in the church, the Rev. Clarence Woods, developed a relationship in Christ at an early age, but he says his faith and trust in God was deepened some 30 years ago when his home burned down to the ground, leaving him, his wife, and two children with absolutely nothing.

"I was pastoring my first church in El Dorado, Arkansas," Woods recalled. "I had a wife and two children and expecting another one. I was what they call a poor pastor, financially. The church I was pastoring at the time didn't believe in paying the preacher, but God had called me to preach and pastor, so I had to do what God had led me to do. God promised me that He would always take care of me. I trusted and believed Him."

But one Saturday morning in 1988, Woods had just finished preaching an 11 o'clock funeral and was on his way to his mother-in-law's home in Camden, Arkansas, about 35 miles away.

"I received a phone call from one of my brothers saying I needed to come back home because my house was burning down," Woods said, before adding, "I hurried back, and when we got there, there wasn't anything left of my home except the blocks."

I didn't have insurance on my home, so we lost everything. We didn't have anything except the clothes we had on our backs that day...

"That day I was in a hopeless situation," said Woods, who was 38 years old at the time. "I didn't have anywhere to take my family. I didn't have anything for them. At that moment, God began to intervene. Here's what happened: there was a guy that

I knew, he was a local assistant fire chief, and he began to pour into us. He gave us six 100 dollar bills. Then I went to my parents' house with my children and my wife, Jackie. When we got there, the assistant fire chief's wife called me and said she wanted to take my wife and children shopping. She went and purchased a brand new wardrobe for my wife and children. This is how God began to work."

Woods said the next day (Sunday) after his home burned down; he preached as he normally did at his church with the suit he had on the day before at the funeral. That suit was the only thing that he owned since he and his family lost everything in the fire the day before.

"The church, at the moment, opened up and gave us furniture so we would have furniture whenever we were able to get a house," Woods revealed. "That same day, there was a lady that I taught in evangelism class, her husband had a rental house, and they told us that we could live in it for six months free rent. All of this happened on that Sunday, a day after our home burned down."

That day, I had money, I had a house to live in, and I had furniture for when I was able to own my own home again....

"That was God," Woods stressed. "God was just moving. Later on that same week, on Tuesday, local pastors in the community called me and said they were going to have a benefit for me on that Saturday of that week. They had a benefit service for me. They received lots of money, and they gave it all to my family."

Woods noted that although God has done many things in his life, he just wants to share with people that when they trust God, not knowing what the future holds, God will provide.

I was able to move into a house larger than what we had, and we had more clothes and more money than we had before our home burned down...

"The only thing that we lost were some memories of things we had in the house, but God provided for us within a week's time," said Woods. "God had given us more than we had in our life and that's a testimony to trusting God and being obedient to God when things may seem bleak, but if you live and be obedient and do what God is calling you to do, no matter what the circumstances look like, God will provide in your time of need. I'm a living testimony, and my family is a living testimony that God provided for us when we couldn't provide for ourselves, simply because we trusted in Him. We had faith. I praise God today for that testimony because He proved to me that He is worthy of trusting and I would tell anyone that if you trust God, you'll sleep well at night because God will provide."

I'M DEBT-FREE

LORETTA HENDRIX
Little Rock, Arkansas

Loretta Hendrix has been an educator for more than 30 years, teaching students the importance of reading, but she says it's what she read in the Bible about money and debt that has allowed her to live a life free of stress and without worry.

"My testimony is that I have had the faith to live a simple, debt-free life," Hendrix said.

Living life free of debt is something that the majority of society says they want for themselves, but in reality, according to an American Psychological Association's Stress in America report, more than 90 percent of Americans say they're stressed about money and debt.

Living in a culture where friends, family, and society itself encourages debt and or living above personal means, Hendrix says it can be hard to commit to living a simple life. But she says that by placing her faith in God to would provide her with everything that she needs, she is free to live her life not burdened by debt.

Hendrix, who lives in a 1,000-square-foot bungalow, home is paid off, and she hasn't had a car note since 1982...

"I am thankful every day for what I have, and I don't concern myself with what others have," Hendrix said, before adding, "I concentrate on what God has done for me and my life. My faith is based on the principle that I live in simple ways because I believe that when you live in ways other than simplicity, you actually lose sight of God's presence and you lose His voice. Scripture says that the people of the Lord know His voice. I believe that in my life, by keeping it simple, it keeps me close to God. I have very little stress. I have reasonably good health, and that's a blessing. It is because of my faith that I am content with where I am in my life and the few assets that I own."

Hendrix says living a simple life, free of worry, and debt is something that anyone can have. God, Hendrix says, wants us to be in a position to hear from Him and to serve people in His name, not in bondage to payments. Instead, He wants us to have freedom and options, something that's usually not an option while in debt.

"You just have to have the faith to step out and make the decision to live a simple life, and having a happy life, something that can be achieved without going into debt," Hendrix said. "This is my testimony that it can be done."

CHAPTER 7
DEATH

MY MOM DIED IN A CAR ACCIDENT WHEN I WAS 17 YEARS OLD, BUT I WAS ABLE TO EXPERIENCE JOY IN A BAD SITUATION

BRANDON R

Plano,

n October 1997, Brandon Rich, a 17-year-old senior in high school was on his way home from football practice expecting to see his mom just as he always did. But this time his mother was not there. And the news that followed not only tested his faith but changed his life forever.

"My mom was a stay-at-home mom, so when she wasn't home, it was something highly unusual," Rich recalled. "My brother and sister, who were in elementary school at the time were across the street with a neighbor. The neighbors came over and told me that my mom was in an accident, but they didn't tell me the degree of the accident."

Rich, however, later learned that his mother was killed in the car accident. She was less than a mile away from home.

"She was hit by a dump truck," Rich revealed. "The driver, who was doing construction work on a tollway in Dallas had tried to stop at a light, but the brakes failed, an accident happened, and she died. This is a time in my life when I had to really rely on faith to get me through it."

Rich went on to note that his mom and biological father divorced when he was young, but his mother remarried when he was six years old. This, according to Rich, would later prove to an invaluable relationship in which he believes was divinely orchestrated. After his mom remarried, Rich was legally adopted.

"From that point on, I grew up in the faith and became a believer, a Christ follower," Rich said. "I had my normal battles with faith in middle school and high school, but when it comes to your mom passing away, looking back, there is no way possible that I could have dealt, grieved, and persevered through that time period without having such a strong faith built up at that time."

> *When a life event like this happens, a lot of people ask the question, why did this happen to me? Why her? She was a great person, a great wife, a mother, everything that you can imagine. They start blaming God...*

"But the perspective I had at the time is that I was grateful for 17 years that I had with her, where my brother and my sister only had nine and six years with her, so being able to see the good in a bad situation, God really shined a light to be able to see that during this difficult time," Rich said. "It really shined a light on how you can see the joy for yourself that I got to spend 17 years with her. To have the perspective of if I had not been raised in the church, and if she had not remarried the man that she did, I would not have been able to deal with it. Even when difficult things happen in my life today, trying to see that there is still joy in difficult times is what I do and the faith in God that I hold on to. During the moment of difficult times, it's tough, but there is joy to be found."

Through faith in Christ, Rich says he was even able to experience joy during his mother's funeral.

"The number of people that were there at the funeral, you could see God's work in all of that, just because of the joy in the lives that she touched throughout her life," Rich said. "The strength of my friends, my faith, and with having good friendships within my high school, and them being Christ followers as well really helped. I thank God and praise Him for the blessings growing up and being raised in the church. I pray for those people that do go through difficult times because not having a relationship with Christ just makes it even more difficult because people can go years grieve-stricken, and can't get on with their lives because of the situation. But I'm a testimony that having a relationship with Christ; they can have a fulfilled life in which Christ wants for them."

"

I BURIED MY HUSBAND ON OUR 50TH WEDDING ANNIVERSARY, BUT GOD...

CONSTANCE SIMS
Atlanta, Georgia

For Constance Sims, life is so much more fulfilling when you have someone to share it with. That's why she says burying her husband on their 50th wedding anniversary was the hardest thing she has ever had to do. She says that it was only her faith in Jesus Christ that brought her through it.

"I buried my husband on December 26, 2003," Sims said of her husband, Frank, who she met in Hogansville, Georgia, when she was 16 years old. "We didn't plan it to happen like this; it just happened to work out that way; that God would call him home a few days before our 50th anniversary. He died of cancer. We had a good life together, a good home, and our faith in Christ kept us together for all of those years."

Sims went on to note that being married for 50 years is a testimony for other married couples today, which by having faith in God, married couples can make it through anything that life throws their way.

"When problems came, by placing our faith in God, we were able to work out our problems," Sims stressed, before adding, "I relied on God's leadership to help us when we needed help. We experienced hardships, trials, and tribulations from the first year of our marriage, but we continuously prayed for God to make things better, and He did. We learned that for our marriage to make it, we had to continuously live and grow together."

As to the secret to of staying married and being in love, Sims says, "there is no secret. Trusting the Lord, placing your faith in Him, and making Him the center of it all, is the only way. I've lived a good life. We had a good life, and although it hurt when Frank died, God was there to help me. He'll help you too."

MY SON WAS KILLED IN 1991, BUT NOW I HAVE CHRIST'S PEACE THAT SURPASSES ALL UNDERSTANDING

DORIS WALLER
Holly Springs, Mississippi

Doris Waller will never forget the day that she got the phone call that no parent ever wants to receive: the news that her 27-year-old son, Darryl R. Waller, had been shot and killed. The day was October 15, 1991.

"I just fell apart," Waller recalled, before adding, "I just lost it. I didn't believe it. I started screaming, and it just didn't seem real. Every muscle in my body was tight."

Waller said following the death of her son, she went into a state of depression, visiting her son's grave every day for six weeks. The funeral director who buried her son heard about Waller's daily routine. He reached out and advised her to stop going to her son's grave on a daily basis because he felt it was only making her feel worse and that she needed to find a source of healing.

Waller heeded to the funeral director's words and drew on the only thing she knew was powerful enough to help.

I decided to put my faith in Christ...

"That was a really rough time for me; I asked the Lord for peace," Waller recalled. "I asked Him for restoration. I asked Him to provide me with His peace that surpasses all understanding. He answered my prayer, and I finally got to a point to where I'll never forget what happened to my son, but I made it to a point to where I could live with it."

Waller says she is a living witness for anyone who has ever lost a loved one as tragic as she lost her son, that there is peace through faith in Jesus Christ.

"Just ask Christ for the peace that you need, and He'll give it to you," Waller said.

I GREW IN FAITH WHILE CARING FOR BOTH OF MY AILING PARENTS

RONALD W

Suga

For Ronald Williams, seeing both of his parents health decline was one of the hardest things he has ever had to deal with, but he says his faith in Christ provided him with the strength he needed when his mother passed away. This was the same time in which his father was hospitalized after having a stroke.

"My mother started to deal with memory issues that developed into a serious type of dementia," Williams said. "As her condition became more challenging, and my dad became less and less able to address them, she eventually had an in-home accident, a fall, where she had to be hospitalized. The lengthy hospital stay was real tough on all of us, and ultimately, she never really recovered from that fall. She passed away in 2012."

During the last few of months of her life, Williams said he watched with difficulty, as his father attended to her on a daily basis.

"He was really stretching himself, he would speak to her while she was in a semi-conscious to an unconscious state," Williams recalled. "He was there reading to her, singing to her, and just doing all he could to try to keep her engaged in some way or another, hoping to bring her out. But while trying to attend to her, he himself had a stroke. My mother went into hospice care while my father was getting treatment for the stroke. Eventually, she passed away."

I often reflect on the spiritual significance of this period of my life...

"My faith grew stronger as a result of this painful and lengthy period," Williams said, before adding, "Ultimately, I believe it made my family stronger. One of the things that stands out the most in terms of a faith lesson is that on an intellectual level, we know that we as people control so very little in our lives. But it becomes really apparent when you're dealing with an ailing loved one, especially like a parent, and it reinforced in me so much of why faith in God is so important. All of the ups and downs and the challenges, successes that you have in life, how they occur, and how they'll impact you, those things are completely unpredictable, so you have to have some stabilizing faith that will guide you through what otherwise will be a very chaotic period."

Williams went on to point out that although this was a difficult time for him and his family, looking back at it, it's something he sees was planned by God.

"I retired in 2011," Williams noted. "However, a year later, my parents, who have always been able to take care of themselves, started to need help. But little did I know that my retirement was going to give me an opportunity to be with my parents, to be there for them, and address their needs in a way that there's no way I could have done had I still been under obligations from a job. It was unforeseeable to me, but it was though it was planned, but not by my own planning, so I give that credit to God. After the fact, it's clear to me what a benefit it was for me to be available for them when their needs were increasing."

It gave me a chance to reflect and take a moment to fully appreciate both of my parents...

"I've always honored and appreciated them, but as they became more dependent on my brothers and me, it allowed me to fully appreciate all the effort they put into raising us, and how they had to go through this exact same thing with their own parents," Williams stressed. "As they would always say, they did it depending and leaning on God. My testimony for others is that when you think about getting weary, you can fall back on the fact that others have come and passed through this way."

This difficult time also helped Williams focus his attention more on his family, friends, and community.

"I've increased my council to my family on the commandment that we received to love your neighbor as yourself," Williams said. "I think it really starts with family and those that God has already placed closest to us in our lives. Those are the ones that we should be serving and loving in accordance with that commandment. This really started to become clearer to me as I went through this period with my parents. We're still taking care of my dad. He is over 91 years old. He is still a deacon at his church, and people are looking out for him beyond us, and that strengthens my brothers and me as well. My family and I were able to get through this time in our lives, but it was through our faith in Christ. Faith is the way that others can get through a time like this too."

"WHEN MY MOM DIED, I DIDN'T THINK I COULD MAKE IT, BUT WITH GOD, I DID

PATRICIA BOGA
Holly Springs, Mississippi

When Patricia Boga's mother, Effie Boga, died of cancer on December 11, 2004, Patricia didn't think she could go on living, but she says it was her faith in Christ that strengthened her and says now she is able to do all things through Him.

"I leaned on my mother for everything," Boga said. "She helped with my daughter, and the rest of my family's children, so when she died I thought I just couldn't make it without her."

Boga, like everyone on earth, will at some point in their lives experience death and tragedy.

"This was the hardest thing that had ever been presented in my life, to know that she had cancer," Boga stressed. "When the doctor informed us, he let us know that he had performed surgery on my mother, but noted that cancer had spread into some areas that he wasn't able to reach."

Boga said the doctor's plan was to place her mother through chemotherapy treatments.

"I was working two jobs at the time, a full-time job and a part-time job as a gospel MC," Boga said. "I was going all around hosting gospel programs and working on the radio (on-air personality). I had to stay strong and hold on to God. There were times where I had to leave work to make sure she had her dinner. I had to take her to chemotherapy sessions at least three or four times a week. I remember times when I would just break down and cry because I saw what she was going through, and I saw how the treatments and cancer were breaking her down. It was so devastating, but I knew I had to be strong because I had to be strong for her."

I had leaned on my mom for so long, but God wanted me to lean on Him...

"All I could do is put my faith in God to help me through this part of my life," Boga said. "It was like once she died, I became the one that my family leaned on, but I had to tell my family that we've been leaning on momma for all of these years, and now God wants us to lean on Him. He wanted to show us that He is the rock and that He is really where our strength comes from. God is a jealous God, and I had to learn to trust Him during a time in which I didn't think I could."

Boga went on to encourage others who have lost a loved one and feels the same way that she felt when her mother died at the age of 78 in 2004.

"It's hard, I know, but my testimony is that I trusted Him and I placed my faith in Christ, and over time, I was able to go on," Boga said, before adding, "This experience has allowed me to get through several other situations in my life. If anyone is going through what I went through, please be encouraged that by placing your faith in Him, you'll make it. You can get through this."

"

MY MOM'S DEATH WAS UNBEARABLE UNTIL I GAVE IT TO GOD

LEROY ROBERTS
Houston, Texas

When Leroy Roberts' mom passed away in 1984, he felt an emotional pain in which he had never felt before, but he says his faith in Christ gave him the strength he needed to get through it.

"I'm a Vietnam veteran, so I have seen a lot, but in 1984 when my mom died, it was the hardest period in my life," Roberts said. "The pain was so unbearable. Also, when she died, my dad was in the hospital dying of cancer, so I had to learn that my mom had died, and go over to the other hospital where my dad was and tell my dad who was dying of cancer that he'd lost his wife and I lost my mom."

I found strength in Jesus

"The day of the funeral, I was so hurt and distraught," Roberts recalled, before adding, "The pain was so unbearable. I was crying, and all I could say is Jesus, Jesus, help me. And I tell you, an unspeakable joy came over me. It was like all of the burdens had been lifted from me."

Roberts went on to encourage anyone who has lost a loved one to place their total faith in Jesus and noted that Jesus would provide them with His peace that surpasses all understanding.

"What I learned on that day, the day that my mom died, is that He was preparing me for the things to come, because as of today, I am 71 years old, and I am the only one in my family to live past 66," Roberts revealed. "My mom died when she was 65. My dad died when he was 66. My oldest brother died when he was 55. My youngest brother died when he was 50, and my brother behind me died when he was 63, so I know that on that day, May 1984, when all I could say is Jesus help me, is that He prepared me for a lot of things to come."

My story is that I have joy...

"I've been blessed," Roberts said. "I've seen a lot, and I know God lives. When someone close to me dies, I am hurt, but I understand that God lives and that we all have an appointed time when we're going to leave this earth. This joy that I have, the world didn't give it to me, and the world can't take it away. I have had prostate cancer. I have had a heart attack, but through faith in God, I was able to make it and live a normal life, so people can't look at me and know my story. I have some good days, and I have some bad days, but my good days always outnumber my bad days. I'm truly grateful for that, and I will always have faith in God, no matter what."

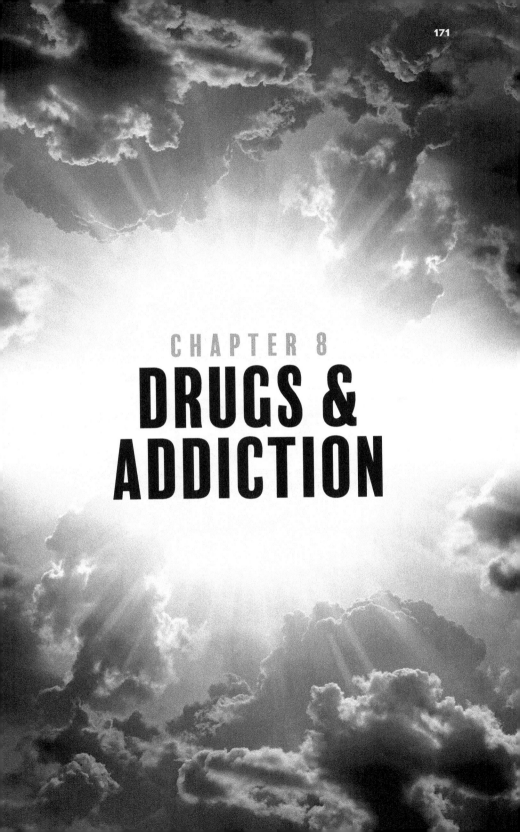

CHAPTER 8
DRUGS & ADDICTION

"I WAS ADDICTED TO DRUGS
FOR 20 YEARS, BUT GOD...

EVELYN BRASS
Houston, Texas

Evelyn Brass always had big dreams for her life. She grew up in the church and developed a love for God at a young age, but some 30 years ago, the dreams she had for her life were derailed when she found herself with the wrong crowd and addicted to crack cocaine.

"I was strung out on drugs for 20 years, from age 28 to age 48," Brass said. "I stayed on crack. I had two children, and they had to go live with my mother because I was just chasing after the drug all the time."

But an arrest for having drug paraphernalia on Feb. 19, 2006, was an event in which Brass says God used to change her life forever. She was walking down the street looking for her next fix. The police, however, stopped her and found her in possession of drug paraphernalia.

"The policeman took me to jail," Brass recalled.

At age 48, Brass, who had never previously been to jail, was facing two years in state prison for possession of drug paraphernalia.

"I went back to my cell, and I prayed to God," she said. "I said, God, if you don't let these people send me to prison, I'll serve you, I'll worship you, I'll teach and preach your Word for the rest of my life. I told God that although I was willing to give my life over to Him, I needed His help, because the way I had been living my life, I knew that people might not accept me. I said God you're going to have to keep opening doors for me and give me a place to stay when I get out of here. I promised God that I would never go back to doing drugs again. When I went back to court, they gave me 60 days in the county jail, but I only actually had to spend 30 days in the county jail."

I got out of jail, and God honored my prayer and started opening one door after another for me...

Brass stressed that her dependence, trust, and faith in God is what allowed her to restore and rebuild her life.

"My message to anyone who has ever been on drugs, been to jail, prison, or a place where it seems like there's no hope for the future, or nothing good can ever happen to them, is that I am a living witness that by trusting and believing in God, anything is possible," Brass said, before adding, "You can be what you want to be, and you can live a happy life, regardless of your mistakes."

Brass said God opened a door for her to attend college at the College of Bible Studies in Houston, where she earned a Bachelor of Science degree in May 2013. God also provided a stable place for her to live and a good job, the two things in which she prayed for while behind bars. But that's not all. Brass enrolled into Houston Baptist University and graduated with a Master of Arts in Theological Studies degree in 2017. She is currently pursuing her doctoral degree.

"God kept me," Brass said. "If He didn't keep me, none of this would be possible, because to tell you the truth, I should not be alive today. God just kept me during my addition. It was nothing that I did. It was all God keeping me. And I believe He took me through that journey for a reason so that I could tell other people how my faith in God saved me from addiction. I just see God's supernatural blessings working right in front of my eyes, and it is awesome. I'm just so glad that God gave me my life back. Out of all the dreams I had for my life, and all of the things that I went through while I was addicted to crack cocaine, I would have never dreamed that my life would ever be this good, thanks to Jesus Christ."

GOD RESTORED MY LIFE AFTER LOSING MY WIFE, CHILD & BUSINESS TO CRACK COCAINE

JACKIE ROGERS
Pascagoula, Mississippi

Jackie Rogers had a life that most people dream of: he was a business owner, the owner of a Domino's Pizza in Tuskegee, Alabama. He was married and had a child, but he says he threw it all away on crack cocaine.

Realizing that his life had spiraled out of control and in of help, Rogers, in 1994, moved to Pascagoula, Mississippi with only two pair of jeans and a worn out pair of Nike's. He moved to The Home of Grace, a faith-based drug and alcohol addiction recovery program that has served South Mississippi for over 50 years.

"After I spent time at the Home of Grace, I had no idea what I was going to do or where I was going to go," said Rogers. "I just knew I didn't want to go back to where I came from. But over time by me sticking with God, keeping the faith in Jesus Christ, God just kind of fixed everything. I didn't know it at the time. I just had to have faith that my life would be fixed."

Upon completing the program at the Home of Grace, Rogers said he needed a way to support himself with a job. For this, he says he placed his trust in God to supply him with one.

"I had to have faith, so I stepped out on faith, and I got a job working as a contractor at Chevron Refinery in Pascagoula," Rogers said. "I remember telling my pastor that I wanted to one day actually work for the company as an employee, so I just kept going to work, doing my job as a contractor, and praying about it."

Rogers, however, didn't stop at simply praying for God to help him. Rogers says he took action by taking the test that is required to become a full-time employee at Chevron Refinery.

"I took the test four times, and I passed the test each time," Rogers said. "The thing is that not only do you have to pass the test, they have to call you. In 2006, I finally got a call saying that I had the job. But God blessed me even more. That same year, I was able to buy a new car. I got a house, and a job, all within a few months. I got a new car in January 2006, a new job in April 2006, and a house in May 2006. It was all because of God and the faith that I had in Him that He would give me back everything that I had smoked up in crack cocaine."

I've been on the job at Chevron for over a decade now...

"I'm now what they call a refinery mechanic, and it's all because of my faith in God," Rogers stressed. "As I look back, I see where it was all in God's plan…not for me to get on drugs, but I had my own business, a wife, a child, and I threw it all away."

Rogers, who is also known at his home church for singing the Gospel song, *If I Had Wings, I'll Fly Away*, said through faith, God has covered his life with His wings of glory.

"I placed my faith in God, and He has restored my relationship back with my daughter," Rogers testified. "I have a cordial relationship with my ex-wife, and by the grace of God, I can now say that I moved from the halfway house to living in my own house."

CHAPTER 9
MILITARY

I SURVIVED FIVE GUNSHOT WOUNDS IN VIETNAM

JAMES LIDDELL
Gary, Indiana

More than 58,220 U.S. military soldiers lost their lives during the Vietnam War, and for James Liddell, he says it's only by the grace of God and his faith in God that he survived the war and is alive and well today.

Liddell served in Vietnam from July 21, 1966, to July 21, 1967.

"While serving in Vietnam, I was wounded nine months after being in the country, which was April 21, 1967, at 9:30 in the morning," Liddell recalled. "We were on patrol going up a mountain, but we ran into an ambush. The Viet Cong had dug inside of the mountains, so we never saw them there."

I was shot five times with an assault rifle...

"Myself and two others were wounded," Liddell said. "My RTO (Radio Telephone Operator) was shot in the neck, and the bullet came out through his back. One of my flank men was shot in the arm. He lost that arm, as a matter of fact."

Had it not been for the grace of God, we all could have gotten killed...

"That day we were supposed to have an air strike, which means our U.S. military was supposed to bomb that mountain before we started to patrol it, but for some reason they called it off, and to this day, I've never known why, and I've never understood why they didn't have the air strike," Liddell stressed. "Of course, being shot five times was very, very painful. It was the most intense pain that I've ever experienced in my life."

After sustaining the five gunshot wounds, Liddell said he laid there wounded for more than an hour while the Viet Cong continued shooting and attacking, "but they never hit me again."

Reinforcements from the United States military eventually arrived.

"Our military helicopters came and shot into the mountains," Liddell said. "I was carried down out of the mountains and put on a helicopter."

Liddell noted that although he was on the helicopter, the nearest hospital was 75 miles away, and making it to that particular hospital with the Viet Cong still in the area, wasn't a sure thing.

"I had no weapons, no nothing," Liddell said. "I was in so much pain, and I was afraid of the helicopter being shot down. They cut off all of my clothing and flew me 75 miles to the hospital, and when I got there, the only thing I had was gauze and an IV, but thanks to God that I was able to make it until they were able to perform surgery."

One of the doctors told me that if one of the bullets were a half inch higher, I would have lost my leg, or if it were a foot higher, I would have been killed...

"As for my wounds, I was shot in the groin area, my leg, buttocks, and abdomen," Liddell said, before adding, "Thanks be to God that I was able to survive that. This experience showed me that we all will go through things in life, but when you put your trust and faith in God into action, He will see you through it. I'm a living witness to it."

THE DAY GOD LET ONE PHONE CALL GET THROUGH

DR. CHAUNCEY DUPREE
Plano, Texas

Some people wonder if God still performs miracles in this day and time, but Dr. Chauncey Dupree says he is living proof that God still does.

"I saw the miraculous move of God," Dupree said. "My military career was up and going, but I was still facing some financial problems. Many people think or are under the impression that the military pays very well and that you make a lot of money serving in the military, which could not be further from the truth. The military is great on benefits for their service members, medical, housing, but the pay scale is really, really low."

The year was 1999. Dupree was serving in the United States Navy at the United States Navy Naval Air Station in Alameda, California, on San Francisco Bay. Like many people can relate to today, his career was going great; however, privately, he was stressed out battling major financial issues.

It seemed like I just could not get on track...

"I wasn't living on base," Dupree recalled. "I had my own home; it was the first house I ever bought. I was facing foreclosure. It had gotten so bad that the electricity and the lights had been turned off because I hadn't paid the bill. The cable and Internet had all been turned off. I just ran into some really bad financial times. I remember thinking, I need to find a part-time job, but here's the problem: it's very hard to work a part-time job and be in the military at the same time. The military is so demanding, specifically depending on the type of job that you do in the military. The type of job I did, aircraft mechanic, it would be really, really difficult to go out and find a part-time job while being full-time in the military."

Dupree said he eventually found a way in which he could squeeze in a couple of hours a day working at night in an effort to get back on track financially.

"I will remember this one particular day for as long as I live, it's my testimony that I tell people, but the funny thing is when I tell other believers, they don't believe me," Dupree said, before adding, "but I was there. I witnessed it with my own eyes, and I will never forget this event. To help provide understanding about my testimony, I have a technical background, where I had done some work on the side in the past with companies like AT&T, so I had learned the telecom industry and how telephone and internet services work.

This one particular day, I went out looking for a part-time job. Back then (1999), you could still go to the place you wanted to work and fill out an application. You could walk into the building and walk right into human resources. You didn't have to fill it out online like you do today. I started early that morning. I went to a total of six places that day, and I heard the same thing over and over—we will call you. I went home very depressed, very down, very low, just feeling like I was at the absolute end of my rope. I mean I had reached my limit."

I remember I told the Lord; I can't take this; this is more than I'm able to bear...

"I didn't know where the money would come from to get the lights turned back on; I didn't know where the money would come from to pay the mortgage, I just didn't know how I was going to pay for anything," Dupree said. "After being out all day long, not hearing anything positive, I was really low, really depressed. And so that evening I sat there on my couch wondering, hoping, thinking, trying to figure out what I was going to do, where I would go tomorrow to fill out more applications, what was I going to do to try to fix this financial issue?"

As I sat there, I remember, I closed my eyes and said a very simple prayer: Lord, here I am...

"And the instant I finished saying that prayer, the phone rang," Dupree said. "Now I know that doesn't sound like a big deal, but here is what's amazing about that: Remember when I said earlier that I had telecom, telephone, and Internet experience, and I knew how it worked? Well, I had cut off enough of other people's phones working for AT&T, etc., to know that when that circuit is cut, that phone does not work. That circuit was cut on my phone. Back then you would pick up the phone, and you wouldn't get the message that the service to this phone has been temporarily discounted. You just wouldn't hear anything, no dial tone, nothing. But the second I finished that brief little prayer, that phone rang. I couldn't believe it. I couldn't believe that the phone was ringing, and the first thing I could think was, wow, they cut my phone back on. Some people may remember that you used to be able to have your phone set up to where it would go to voicemail after so many rings. Well, the phone just kept ringing. It rang about six times, and I hesitated to answer it because I couldn't believe what I was hearing."

Dupree said he answered the phone and low and behold; it was one of the jobs he applied for earlier that day.

"They said, Mr. Dupree, you applied for a position? I said yes," Dupree recalled. "They said you can start on Monday. There was no interview; no come back to fill out more paperwork. They said you can start on Monday. I said that's fantastic. I'll be there on time. I sat there thinking, wow."

That's when I realized God did something supernatural for me...

"I was so excited, I remember thinking I need to call my family, I need to call my mother and let her know what's going on," Dupree noted. "I picked up the phone to call my mother, and it was dead. No service. I realized two things. God allowed one call to get through because people told me that they were trying to call me all day, and they said my phone was off. But out of all the phone calls that were made to me, one call got through. The second thing I learned that day is that what God does in the spiritual, He also does in the physical. Through faith, God let one call get through. That call was the blessing I needed."

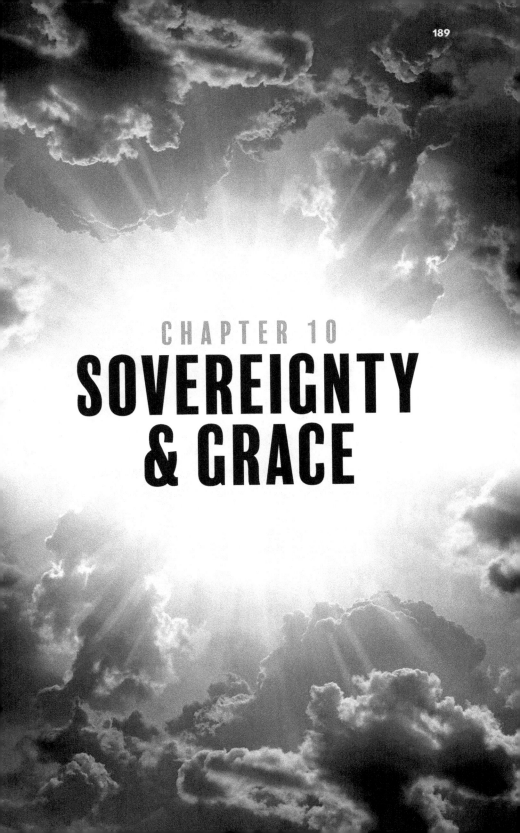

CHAPTER 10
SOVEREIGNTY & GRACE

"FAITH IN THE MIDST OF THE SEPTEMBER 11TH TERRORIST ATTACKS

MICHELLE LLOYD
Sugar Land, Texas

Michelle Lloyd believes that completely trusting God, regardless of the circumstances, is the best decision anyone can make, but she says her faith was tested in a big way when she found herself among the thousands of people affected during the September 11, 2001, terrorist attacks that killed 2,977 people in New York, the Pentagon and in a field in rural Pennsylvania.

"For me, it all started on September 10, 2001," Lloyd recalled. "I was a training officer for JP Morgan Chase, where I trained newly hired investment advisors in the Texas region, and in the cities of Tampa and New York. On this day, I had departed Houston and flew to lower Manhattan, New York, because I had a training class to facilitate there. It was myself, and also a facilitator was my direct report and boss, who was also employed at JP Morgan Chase. This particular day, I arrived at LaGuardia Airport. I took a town car to the World Trade Center Marriott, which was where I typically stay while I'm there. I got settled in, went down into the tunnel, grabbed dinner, and mingled with some friends. At the time, my family, a four-year-old, one-year-old, and my husband, Earl, was back in Houston. I traveled quite a bit for JP Morgan Chase."

This was just a typical trip, so I thought...

The training was a few miles away from the hotel.

"I woke up about 5:30 the next morning, which is pretty early for me," Lloyd said. "The training wasn't until 9:30 or 10 o'clock. I attempted to go back to sleep, but I was unable to go back to sleep, so I decided I would do something different instead of going back down into the tunnel. I decided to do breakfast, so I went down and got a bagel from one of the trucks on the street."

After having breakfast, Lloyd decided to go to the training early and simply wait for the investment advisors to arrive.

"As I was getting into the town car that picked me up, I heard a loud crash," Lloyd reflected. "Of course, I'm in New York, and not in Texas, so I thought that maybe this is something that they have going on here, so I got into the car and reached the training location. When I arrived, I noticed a few people, including my boss, who was looking out of the window.

That's when we saw the second plane hit the Twin Towers...

"At that moment, ambiguity filled the air," Lloyd stressed, before adding, "We were in disbelief, and uncertain of what was going on. I told my boss that I was going to go back to the airport to go home. We said our goodbyes. I got into the car to go to the airport, and it seemed as though traffic had already built up. We were inching, going absolutely nowhere, because by this time debris was falling, people were in disarray, and I was unable to get any reception on my cell phone. It was eeriness in the air. People were walking at a very slow pace; it was like life had stopped."

After a period of time, according to the Lloyd, her driver was able to make some leeway through traffic.

"I looked to my right, and I saw people jumping from the tower," Lloyd said. "Then word had traveled back that no planes were leaving out of New York at all. I asked the driver to try to find another Marriott a little further away from where we were. We started to get a little distance, and as I looked back, I noticed that…

one of the Twin Towers had fallen over the hotel where I had slept...

"I was sure that people were still there at the hotel sleeping," Lloyd said. "I arrived at the next Marriott. I tried to call back home, and I tried to call my boss, but I was unable to due to reception issues. Then I learned that I was on JP Morgan Chase' missing person's list. Later, I had come to learn that my boss had inhaled so much of chemicals from the debris that he had passed away."

Those days I had never spent as much time on my face before God seeking a deeper relationship with Him...

"I already had a relationship with Christ, but I just needed to go deeper with him," Lloyd said. "When I look back at this episode in my life, I think about the faith of those in the Bible like Elijah, Elisha, and Nehemiah. What I noticed in these individuals is they trusted completely in God, not three-quarters of the way, not 90 percent of the way, but they trusted completely in God. Secondly, they encouraged people; they encouraged the hearts of the world towards God and believed in God-sized miracles. My faith in Him during this time is a testimony to Him protecting me, taking care of me, and also what He can do in everyone else's life."

GOD GAVE ME A TRIPLE PORTION OF GRACE, MERCY & FAVOR

MORRIS V. GURNELL, JR.
Indianapolis, Indiana

Morris Gurnell is a living witness that when you put your faith and trust in God, He has the power to deliver you even if you're facing death.

"I was knocking on death's door three times in my life, but with much prayer and faith in Christ, I'm still here alive and well today," Gurnell said. "The first time death was knocking at my door was in 1984. I was 25 years old, living in the south, so I wanted to try gumbo since eating gumbo is a pretty big deal in the south. I ate a bowl of gumbo and ended up with hepatitis."

According to the Centers for Disease Control and Prevention, more than 19,000 people die each year from hepatitis, with approximately 3.5 million Americans living with hepatitis C.

In addition to having hepatitis, I also contracted jaundice...

"I wasn't sure why I was sick at the time, but I got to a point to where I had jaundice, and I was urinating blood," Gurnell explained, before adding that in his illness, turning to the Lord is what saved his life. Lying sick in bed, Gurnell said for strength; he reflected upon Isaiah 38:2, where Hezekiah turned his face to the wall and prayed to the Lord.

"So that's what I did, and my body was healed," Gurnell said. "I turned to the wall, I prayed, and had faith that God would heal my body, and He did."

The second time Gurnell knocked on death's door involved a serious car accident in 2002.

"My car was totaled, and my kids were in the back seat," Gurnell recalled, before adding, "There's no way that any of us should have walked away, but all four of us were able to come out of that accident without having to go to the hospital. The police officer who dealt with us on that particular scene was commending me for having my children on the back seat and in a seatbelt, because just an hour or so before our accident, there was another accident.

The driver involved in that particular accident had placed his son in the front seat, and the impact of the accident sent his son through the windshield. So when I looked back at my car, the fact that no one got hurt, the fact that I still have all three of my children, and they have their father, there's no doubt in my mind that God had a hand in it."

The third time Gurnell knocked on death's door was in 2012. Like many people across the globe, Gurnell wanted to get back in shape, so he signed on with a trainer who had him performing a variety of what he describes as peculiar workouts.

But soon after a few workouts were completed, Gurnell started to feel soreness in his arms.

"My urine was a tea color, so I went to the doctor," Gurnell recalled. "The doctor told me that was normal, but I was doing too much upper body work and that I needed to give my body some rest."

But while Gurnell was there at the hospital, he took a blood test.

"They told me I needed to take a rest and drink a lot of water, however, with me being in the field of education, I was already scheduled to go out of town to a principal's workshop in Austin, Texas, so in my mind, I couldn't take a rest," he said. "I went to the workshop in Austin."

The doctor called with the results of the blood test I took and said I needed to leave the workshop in Austin and get back to the hospital in Houston right away because my kidneys were shutting down...

"When I got home in Houston, my wife took me to the hospital, and when I got to the hospital, they immediately put me in ICU (Intensive Care Unit)," said Gurnell, who was in ICU for four days undergoing three dialysis treatments. "The lady who did the dialysis was a big-time Christian, so she would sing gospel songs to me while I was on dialysis. After four days there, they put me in a private room for further recovery. Everybody was telling me that I was going to be on dialysis for a while. First, they said I needed five treatments; then they said I needed a full year of treatments, then they said I was going to be on dialysis for the rest of my life."

But what I didn't know is that the doctors actually thought I was going to die...

"I devoted many hours in prayer with God," Gurnell said. "All I could do is place my faith in Christ. I trusted Him. I believed that He heard my prayers, and He did. My kidneys kicked back in, and my healing came to pass. At the time, I had no idea that I was knocking on death's door, but the doctors knew it. As I look back at it and the prayers I received and the prayers I personally prayed—as I look at the people God had attending to me, from my nurse to the dialysis person, to my doctor, God had everyone and everything in place for my healing. God had to let me know that there's nothing I can do in my own strength, but through faith in Him, all things are possible."

"

LISTENING TO GOD'S VOICE SAVED MY LIFE

JAYNE WILLIAMS
Beaumont, Texas

L istening to the soft, still voice of God is something that Jayne Williams had always heard about as a child, and it's something that even as an adult, she has taught to the children she teaches on a weekly basis at her local church, but in May 2014, listening to the voice of God proved to be the same principle that saved her life.

"I was in a staff meeting and experienced a headache, which was not uncommon, so I went to the nurse asking for Tylenol," Williams recalled. "For some reason, the nurse told me she wanted to take my blood pressure. My blood pressure was elevated, and from time to time, it gets like that."

Williams proceeded to tell the school nurse that she would simply drink some water, just as she normally would whenever her blood pressure rises.

"I told her that I would rest when I got home because I had a presentation to make at work," Williams said. "For whatever reason, she said no, I want you to sit here, and I'm going to get the principal. The principal came, and I said it was no big deal. They kept insisting, so I said I'll go home. On the way home, I started feeling a little bit differently."

Williams decided to call and check her symptoms with her doctor...

"Normally my doctor is never ever available to see me the same day," Williams said. "She said to come on in. She checked me, and she said you seem to be OK and if you start to feel differently, I want you to call me back."

Later, Williams did start feeling differently. She called her doctor and revealed her symptoms. However, based on her reported symptoms, Williams was told that she did not have to come back to see the doctor.

"Later on that night, something told me, and I felt like it was the Lord, that you need to listen to these people to, you need to maybe go to the hospital," Williams said, before noting, "I'm a person that resists, so I said to myself that I need to do what the Lord is telling me to do. I went to the doctor, the emergency room. I told the doctor about my symptoms. I told them it hurts when I put my head down."

They did an MRI, a CAT scan, and a spinal test, and it came back that I had meningitis....

Williams stressed that after hearing the results, she immediately became fearful.

"I know that meningitis can be a deadly disease, whether it's a virus or a bacterial infection," Williams said.

According to the Centers for Disease Control and Prevention, bacterial meningitis is very serious and can be deadly. Death can occur in as little as a few hours. Most people recover from meningitis. However, permanent disabilities, such as brain damage, hearing loss, and learning disabilities, can result from the infection.

"They had to call a specialist in from the Centers for Disease Control and Prevention," Williams said. "The doctor was quite unsure of the treatment to give me. My mom came, we prayed, and it turned out that I had to stay in the hospital for seven days. They kept trying different medicines. My mom and I continue to pray because the doctor didn't know how much medicine to give me."

I knew that I had to depend on God to heal me...

Williams was ordered by her doctor to stay at home for an additional 10 days, "but the doctor also told me that even after the 10 days that they were still uncertain if that would be enough," Williams said. "Basically, I just felt like I had to rely completely on God because my doctor was unsure. Since meningitis is a disease that can be contagious, and the seriousness of the disease, listening to the voice of God and putting my faith in Him, is what helped me. I had to completely rely on the Lord to heal my body. That is all that I could do, and I'm blessed to be here today because of it. My testimony to others is that listening to God, trusting Him, and putting your faith totally in Him is the best thing to do. I am living proof that things will turn out for your good if you do."

"

I LISTENED TO GOD'S VOICE &
NOW MY LIFE IS MUCH BETTER

JOHNNY KING-SMITH
Atlanta, Georgia

The year was 2006. Johnny King-Smith had been dealing with a variety of health issues and was ready for a permanent solution, a solution in which medicine nor doctors could provide, but she says once she started listening to the voice of God, she was able to get the results she so desperately needed.

"I had been going to this doctor for a while, and I had started noticing that when I would tell them things, they were not listening," Smith said, before adding, "So I started praying. I said Lord make it plain to me. If it's time to make a change, please let me know. Show me, and make it simple beyond a shadow of a doubt that a child would even know. The next time that I went to that particular doctor, there were some things that I had already told him that I was allergic to, and it would cause me to have a reaction in the form of a severe headache. He didn't listen. He prescribed something similar to what I am allergic to. Sure enough, once I took a dose of it, I had the worse headache that there ever was."

Smith said she prayed and asked God for direction.

God revealed that it was time to switch doctors...

Smith listened to the voice of God and changed doctors. Since that time in 2006, Smith, who has battled with various health issues over that past decade, has experienced an improvement in her overall health.

"Sometimes you have to stand on faith and trust the voice of God and know that He is with you in the midst of the fight, and that He will bring you out victorious," King stressed, before adding, "The Bible says to stand still and watch the salvation of the Lord, and watch the Lord work. I've had to stand still in a lot of situations of my life and watch the salvation of the Lord work. I can testify that He is still in control."

Smith went on to note that "If there's anything you're faced with, something you're praying about, and you're looking for an answer, just know that all you have to do is have faith in Him, stand still, and watch the hand of God move in your life. That's what He did for me, and He will do the same for you too."

GOD WAS THERE FOR ME RIGHT WHEN I NEEDED HIM THE MOST

MAXINE RICHMOND

Holly Springs, Mississippi

Maxine Richmond learned early on in life what it means to be a Christian. A Christian, she says, is supposed to lean not to his or her own understanding, but to lean on God. Leaning on God is exactly what she had to do during several events throughout her life, a reason why she says God has provided comfort for her every time she needed it.

"As a young girl in the church, I would listen to stories on how people leaned on God," Richmond said. "I have leaned on Him at various stages of my life."

The greatest help was when my husband became ill with a stroke; Blood clots got all in his way...

He died on June 5, 2016.

"God made it to where I didn't have to go through this by myself," Richmond stressed, before adding that regardless of what she was going through in her life, God would always send her the comfort she needed, right when she needed it.

"God would always calm me down," Richmond said. "I'm an emotional person, and sometimes I would be screaming in reaction to things going on in my life, but all of a sudden, a calmness would come to me."

Her testimony of faith, she says, is that she has learned to wait upon the Lord and advises that anyone who is going through something to do the same thing.

"God loves all of us, and if you would be patient and wait on Him, He'll send comfort," Richmond stressed. "That's how God worked in my life; by being there when I needed help when I didn't know where to go or what to do. He sent people to help me. I listened to the people who helped me. God places people in your life to help show you where you need to go. Losing my husband was one of the hardest things I have ever had to deal with, but through faith in God, I have the peace that surpasses all understanding. He'll do the same for anyone else, but the key is to trust Him by faith."

THE SOVEREIGNTY OF GOD

Losing a loved one is never easy, but experiencing the death of someone close to you for the very first time can cause anyone to wonder how to go on. But Emma Roberts says when her mom died in 1990, it was her faith in God's sovereignty that provided her with what she needed to get through it.

The Sovereignty of God is the biblical teaching that all things are under God's rule and control and that nothing happens without His direction or permission. Romans 8:28 says that all things work together for good to those who love God, to those who are called according to His purpose.

"There comes a time when you have to develop a personal faith walk with the Lord, and I remember it vividly; it was 1990 when my mother past," Roberts recalled. "At this point in 1990, I had never experienced a break or loss amongst my core member family. This was the first experience for one of the core members of my family to pass, and proved to be a defining moment in my faith walk."

Roberts was getting ready for work one morning in 1990 when she received a phone call that her mother had been rushed to the hospital because of a severe headache. In response, Roberts said she quickly traveled from Houston to Beaumont, approximately 85 miles away.

"I remember praying as I never had before, specifically talking to God and praying and entrusting my mother to Him," Roberts recalled. "My mother and I and my sister were extremely close. I knew He would not take my mother unless it was her time. I remember truly feeling a sense of peace after I prayed, even though I knew that she might not make it."

My mom was in grave condition; she had an aneurysm to rupture...

"It was during that pivotal experience that I knew, I really knew I had to trust God," Roberts said, before adding, "Losing a loved one is never easy, but there were two things that God really impressed upon me: You don't have to be sick to die. We as humans really already know this, but until you actually experience that deeper pain of losing someone you're extremely close to, and you're not prepared—not that you can become fully prepared to lose someone, it becomes very real. It impacted me in a new and different way."

The second thing that Roberts said she gained from the experience of losing her mother is that we have to trust God with everything in life.

"You pray to Him," Roberts stressed. "As I prayed that prayer, saying that I'm entrusting my mother to you, He impressed upon me that just like I trust Him in life, I have to trust Him in death because He is truly sovereign. That experience really began my deeper yearning for me to know God's word, to apply it to my everyday life, that He is truly sovereign."

Roberts said losing her mother is a testimony of faith that she had to trust God even when she couldn't see what life would be like without her mother. She went on to encourage others who have experienced loss of a loved one, and those who will lose loved ones in the future to know that placing their faith in God will provide the peace that's needed to go on living.

"We don't always have to like what He does, but we must learn to trust Him and accept that He is sovereign," Roberts said. "For me, He is the author of life and death, and I have learned to trust His timing."

"GOD HEALED MY SON'S HEART CONDITION & HAS SHOWN FAVOR TO MY DAUGHTER

CHANDRA DONALD
Houston, Texas

Experiencing God's favor in your own life is one thing, but experiencing His favor in the lives of your children is, according to Chandra Donald, a totally different thing. But she credits it to having the faith to speak the word of God over the lives of both of her children while they were still in her womb.

"God has been faithful in blessing my seed," Donald said. "When my husband and I got married, we made the decision that when we had our children that they would grow with us as we grew in God."

Both her daughter, Jasmine, and son, James, have done exactly that.

"In the womb, we used to pray over our kids and speak the word of God over our kids," Donald said. "When I was pregnant with them, we would thank God for their gifts, thank God for who they were. We called them by name. My daughter is the grace of God in action for me. I call her my grace because God has always been gracious to her. He has always been sufficient for everything that she has needed. Even as a child when she needed things during times when we were in a struggle and couldn't get the things she needed, God always made a way for her. Even now, she is growing in the ministry. In fact, she was named the national evangelism coordinator for the national organization called InterVarsity."

InterVarsity, which has 1,015 chapters on 687 college campuses in the United States, the mission is to minister to students and faculty through small group Bible studies, large group gatherings, leadership training, thoughtful discipleship, and life-changing mission trips. Its vision is to see students and faculty transformed, campuses renewed, and world changers developed.

"In addition to this, my daughter is also the evangelism coordinator at Prairie View A&M University, which was birth from a ministry she established her freshman year in college," Donald said. "Her growth and faith in God truly inspire me. However, I know that it's the faith that I had to show in Christ in order for all of this to happen."

While Donald calls her daughter her grace, she says her son is her sunshine, someone who she says God has healed of several health-related issues.

"James truly illuminates my day, my life, and it's just a blessing to have such an amazing worshipper in our home," said Donald. "He is a very humble child. He lives in a state of faith that is beyond even my imagination. He has gone through a series of health issues that we usually don't speak about because of his faith and because of what he has shared with us."

The first health-related issue happened during the 2012-2013 school year when James was in the fifth grade...

"He was playing little league football, and he was hit by two young men on the football field, a head-on collision," Donald recalled. "He was knocked out in total blackness on the field. He had a concussion. It was a hairline fracture on his brain. He was put on a regimen for six weeks to heal his concussion. My son was obedient, to not watch TV, he couldn't go to choir practice, and he couldn't play video games. He had to actually rest his brain. We thank God for that because God healed his concussion."

The second health-related issue happened during the 2014-2015 school year, his seventh-grade year.

He went to get a physical for football, and during the physical, the doctor discovered that he had an irregular heartbeat…

"We were told immediately that he had to see a cardiologist," Donald explained. "He had a condition where his left ventricle was closing, and the valve was actually closing. It was, according to the doctor at that time, something he was born with, something that he already had, but we just did not know it. When we were driving from the doctor's office, my son could not see me, but I was crying and praying to God about what we were facing."

But when she and her family arrived at home, Donald said James, surprised her with what he did as an act of faith in God, an act in which she says ended up being an act of faith for their entire family.

"We asked him if he wanted us to place his name on the prayer request at church. He said, no, we're going to call granny and paw, paw into the living room, and as a family, we're going to pray," Donald said. "He was a seventh grader leading us in prayer. He said we're not going to speak it. We're not going to share it with anybody. We're just going to pray and believe God. He started the prayer, and thanked God for full healing, and said that we would not speak a word of it from that day forward. At that moment in my life as his parent, his mother, I had to place my total faith in God and go on as if the victory was already done."

When we went back to the cardiologist, the cardiologist had James' EKG in his hand, and he had his nurse run a new EKG, but after he ran it, he was really baffled by the results…

"He said, I don't understand because I'm seeing what we saw previously, your prayers must have been working, and your God must be an awesome God," Donald recalled the doctor saying in amazement. "He looked at my son and said you have a heart of a champion. Your heart is perfect. I'm looking at the reports, and this is not the same heart. He told him that day that you're clear. I'm going to let you wear a monitor for 30 days just to verify before you play any sports. And after the 30 days, he cleared my son with a full bill of health. That was a major triumph."

Donald said her testimony to others is that placing your faith and children in God's hands and believing and trusting that God will make a way for them even when it looks like there is no way gives God the opportunity to do the miraculous in their lives.

"We have to take God at His word," Donald stressed, before adding, "We believe in praying God's word back to Him. God's word says by His stripes we are healed. My son was healed. We serve an awesome God. He is the author and finisher of our faith. Regardless of what you're going through, we have a real-life testimony that God is real."

"

I LIVED IN A TRASH CAN AS A CHILD, BUT GOD...

ANTONIO SMITH, JR.
Galveston, Texas

L ife has never been easy for Antonio Smith, especially as a child, but he says he is living proof that by faith, God can take a negative situation, and turn it into something positive.

"My parents were forced to give me up at six years old due to abuse," Smith said. "By the time I was six years old, I found myself homeless, and I had to live inside of a dumpster located about three blocks away from the place that I lived. My parents were crack addicts. I was left homeless, and so here I am in this trash can. I failed the fifth grade. I failed the sixth grade, I starved every day, and I had to put myself through school just to eat."

Thinking back on the years he lived in the trash can, from age six to age 14, Smith said he remembers looking up every night admiring the blinking stars in the sky.

"But one day I realized that the blinking stars were actually planes going over my head," Smith recalled, before adding, "Over and over I would look at those stars, and look at those planes, and I would visualize me being in those planes traveling the world because it was a lot better than me being in the trash can with mosquitos and bugs."

Smith, who was adopted at age 14, and aged out of CPS custody when he turned 18, said that trusting God by faith and depending on God to lead and guide him to his ultimate destination was one of the best things that he could have ever done for himself.

As a result, today, God has allowed me to travel the world on those same planes I admired as a kid living in a trash can," Smith said. "It was all because of the faith I had in God and that fact that I had a picture of where I wanted to go. My testimony is that God jumped inside of my picture, and has allowed me to get on those planes and out of that trash can."

Today, Smith is the founder of ATS Jr. Companies, a consulting firm that teaches clients from across the globe that if they can see it, and have enough faith, God will take them there.

"I started in a trash can, I ended up on a plane, and all I do today is teach people how to get out of their personal trash can situations, and how they can get on whatever planes that they have in their lives," Smith stressed. "God literally took me out of a trash can. As a child, I wasn't able to afford gas money or lunch money, but today, I have a passport."

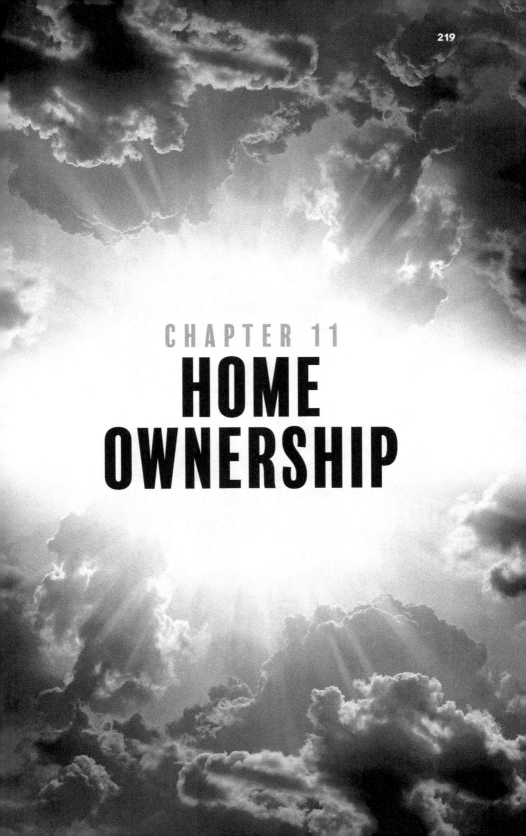

CHAPTER 11
HOME OWNERSHIP

GOD GAVE ME
THE PERFECT HOME

NORMA E. SCARBOROUGH
University Park, Illinois

Like any mother, Norma Scarborough always wanted to be able to provide a loving home for herself and her daughter, but she says that looking at her circumstances in the spring of 1993, it was only through faith that she was able to purchase the perfect home.

"I was a widow living in an apartment, and I had a deep desire to live in my own home, but my credit wasn't good enough to get approved for a home loan," Scarborough recalled. "I was applying for homes costing between $55,000 to $60,000, but all of the banks kept turning me down."

But I knew that with God, all things are possible...

Psalms 37:4 says, "Delight yourself in the Lord, and He will give you the desires of your heart."

Scarborough said that's exactly what she did, delight herself in the Lord. As a result, she was blessed.

"Despite my credit issues, I still believed that God would grant me the desire of my heart to purchase a home for myself and my daughter," Scarborough said, before adding, "I just went out on faith and trusted that He would allow me to live in a house."

Scarborough said a soon as she gave her circumstances totally up to God, that's when it seemed as if the windows of heaven were opened for her.

"I was approached about a house that was $79,000 in Richton Park, Illinois, but since I had already been turned down by banks for homes for $20,000 less than this home, I didn't see how I could ever be approved to live in the home," Scarborough said. "When I saw the house, it was simply beautiful, perfect, just what we needed, three bedrooms and one and a half baths."

Within a three-month span, God made the impossibility of me purchasing a home, possible...

"I decided to just go on faith, and despite my credit issues, despite the fact that I had already been turned down for homes that cost a lot less than this one, I applied for the home loan hoping for God to grant me the desire of my heart, and He did. I got approved, and I was able to purchase the home for my daughter and I. I started this process in the spring of 1993 when I couldn't get approved for a home loan, but once I put it in God's hands, within three months, I was approved for my home. I realized that when I was getting turned down, I was actually just settling because of how badly I wanted to be able to purchase my own home, but God didn't want me to settle. He wanted to give me the desire of my heart, the perfect home for my daughter and I. My testimony for others who, just like me, have a desire to live in your own home but your individual circumstances say otherwise, is that by placing your faith in Christ, you don't have to settle. Just believe that He can do it for you and He will. I'm a living witness."

"

I WAS BLESSED TO BUY MY OWN HOME

LEE GIVAN RUTHERFORD
Southaven, Mississippi

F or years, Lee Givan Rutherford had a dream in her heart of buying her own home, but not just any home. She had a very specific one in mind: a home in the Lyon's Gate Community in Southaven, Mississippi, an area where the average home price is over $200,000. But there was a huge problem to overcome for her dream to come true: her credit was ruined.

"I had previously co-signed on things for some of my family members, who didn't pay the bill each month for items they received for themselves with the assistance of my credit, which caused my credit to go bad," Rutherford said. "I am a living witness to anybody who wants to own their own home, but have credit issues that can complicate things, that when you put your trust and faith in God, anything is possible."

> *My credit had gotten lower than the average score, but I knew that with God, getting the home I wanted was still possible...*

The typical credit score of a homebuyer is 728—slightly higher than the national average. Of the 85,369 mortgage applicants surveyed by the Federal Reserve, only 6.8 percent had scores below 620. The average FICO score in America is 695, and the average Vantage score stands at 673. Currently, Fair Isaac Corp's FICO score and Vantage are two of the most widely used scoring models in the country. Both models range between 300 and 850—the higher the score, the better.

Rutherford said that despite all that she was up against, her credit score and the fact that three other credit-worthy individuals also wanted to purchase the same home, she put her faith in God to give her the desire of her heart.

Psalms 37:4: Delight yourself also in the Lord, and He shall give you the desires of your heart

"That's what I did," Rutherford said. "I delighted myself in the Lord, and He answered my prayer. On December 15, 2015, I was blessed with exactly what I wanted, the $200,000 house with four bedrooms, a large living room, and kitchen area."

But that's not all: God blessed me with a new vehicle to drive to and from my new home

"God has been so good," Rutherford stressed, before adding, "He also blessed me with a husband in 2016. During my journey to purchase my home, I just decided to stop complaining so much and just put my trust and faith in God. After I did that, He blessed me with my home, and then some. With God, there is hope."

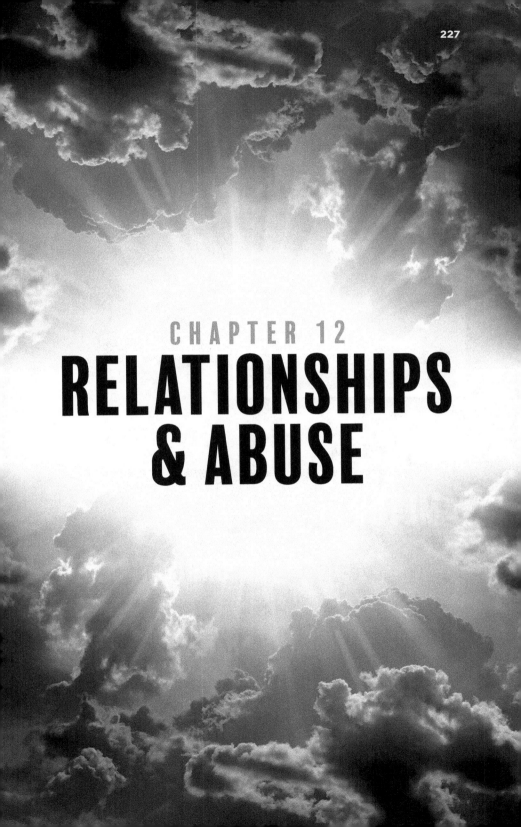

CHAPTER 12
RELATIONSHIPS & ABUSE

#METOO

CHRISSY CAREW
Boston, Massachusetts

Then #MeToo movement sweeping across the United States and abroad caused *Time Magazine* to name Silence Breakers as Person of the Year 2017, but more than 20 years before this movement was birth, Chrissy Carew, says she too experienced sexual misconduct and says it was her faith in God that allowed her to get through it.

"I am telling a story that I've never told publicly before," Carew revealed in an interview January 2018. "I'm doing this so that I can properly support other women."

The #MeToo movement that's filling Twitter, Facebook, and Instagram with stories from sexual assault survivors have been felt around the world as thousands of people, mostly women and some celebrities, declared their solidarity all the way to the U.S. Supreme Court when Justice Ruth Bader Ginsburg revealed that she too is a victim.

When a Christian is sexually violated and has to rely on their faith in God

The year was 1994, Carew had aspirations of becoming a professional speaker and personal coach to empower others in finding their purpose and achieve success in every area of their life. To ensure that she had all of the tools, knowledge, and capabilities to help others, she enrolled in a class that specialized in developing speakers and coaches.

"I was sexually violated by my mentor, and I was very shocked by it," Carew recalled.

He was someone I looked up to—someone I thought was my champion and advocate and had my best interests at heart...

"I had missed one of the classes, and he invited me to come and view it on video right before our next class started, so I was there probably two hours before the rest of the class," Carew recalled.

I started watching the video, he came over in front of me and started pleasing himself; It was quite shocking and then he started to molest me...

"I was in such shock that I couldn't move," Carew said, before adding, "I was stunned. People came into the class. I actually stayed for the class. I can't believe I did that, but I was in such shock. After the class, I left. I went home. I hid under the covers. My husband was working that night, and I pretended I was asleep when he came home because I didn't want to tell him. I didn't want to upset him."

Carew said she was so upset by the events that had occurred that on that day she developed hives from head to toe.

"I knew I had to tell him," Carew said, referring to her husband, who she had been married to for two years at the time of the incident. "When I told him, I was really afraid that this person who violated me, who had a lot of brothers, would somehow hurt my husband. I don't know why I was afraid of that."

I was traumatized...

For help, Carew said she visited a local priest.

"I called the priest, and that was really helpful to be with him," Carew said. "He was a wonderful priest who I will forever love."

Carew noted that she was so traumatized that it took her a month before she actually drove to the police station to report the crime in person. She said her experience at the police station was the opposite of what she ever expected. To my surprise, the policewoman I reported it to was very discouraging and not at all supportive like I thought she would be ... especially because she was a woman.

"I had heard stories about when women come forward, that they're really torn apart, and not taken seriously, and now that it was me going through it, I discovered for myself that it was so true, but I had to go, I had to go," Carew said.

I had to get down on my knees and ask God to give me the courage to go...

She noted that one of her reasons for going to the police was because there was a young girl in her class, and she was so afraid that her mentor could potentially sexually violate her as well.

"So I don't think I did it for myself, I did it for others," Carew stressed, before adding, "I just wanted to make sure that he didn't have the opportunity to do it again to anyone else. The police filed the report, and I went into therapy because it was so shocking to me. In the meantime, my father was dying. I'm very close to my parents, and this was the first time in my whole life where I didn't want to share what happened to me. I just didn't want to burden them with it. My husband was wonderful. I even told my stepchildren. I was afraid that this perpetrator, who worked with someone very famous; I was afraid that this would somehow get out and they were going to try to slam my name, so I felt like I had to tell the children just in case that happened, which was torture for me to share that with the kids."

It was really tough...

Carew said the next step was for her to attend a hearing where the judge would decide whether or not her case would go to trial.

"The judge said this is going to court," said Carew, who was 41 years old at the time. "Court was horrific, just like I heard. His lawyer said all kinds of things that were not true, and they make the women out to be a floozy, which was not true. On the last day of court in the spring of 1994, which I lost, my husband and I were driving home. My father, at this point, was in the VA hospital for good. He had dementia, and my husband said let's stop by and see your dad, and I said I don't think I'm up for it. My husband talked me into it, and I'm so glad I went because my father died the next morning. So I put on a happy face for him, and I know that he would have been really proud of me for stepping forward in honor of other women and particularly the young girl."

I didn't realize it until years after the incident happened, that I hadn't totally healed from it...

"I was in a business situation where I felt betrayed by business people, and I noticed that I was using language like betrayal, I feel violated," Carew said. "That made me realize that I needed to do more work on this sexual violation because those words, those feelings wouldn't come out if I was healed and so I went back to therapy," Carew said. "That's very important. It really hits you at your core when you're violated. But my faith in God played a huge role in healing. I had to depend on Him, and I'm really glad I did. It really gave me a lot of peace. I thank God for giving me the courage to go through this. Even though I lost in court, which the police said I would, I'm glad I did it, because at least there is a record that this happened. And if he ever does it again, there will be a record there that he has gone to court previously on this issue."

The blessing is that it has made me so much more compassionate and loving toward other people...

"That's the gift that came from this," Carew declared. "I can really be with them, be really present, really loving, and have an enormous amount of compassion and an enormous amount of empathy. It is really easy for me to build trust with others. I love that people feel really safe and very supported by me. I feel really grateful for those gifts that came from this horrific incident. My capacity to love is so deep. That is such a gift."

BY PLACING MY FAITH IN GOD, I'M HERE TODAY, A SURVIVOR OF DOMESTIC ABUSE

KIMBERLY CARROLL
Plaquemine, Louisiana

Kimberly Carroll says she has seen God work in the lives of people she knows and in the lives of those she doesn't know, but added that when she needed God to intervened in her life, it was only through faith in Jesus Christ that she was protected and rescued from what's commonly referred to as a quiet epidemic across the globe: domestic abuse.

"Most people who know me, know that I am a cancer survivor, but domestic abuse is something that I did not share because I was ashamed, and I didn't want people to know that this was a struggle that I was going through," Carroll revealed, before adding, "It was quite difficult, and for years I kept the secret."

But she isn't the only one. According to the National Coalition Against Domestic Violence, one in three women, and one in four men have been a victim of physical brutality by an intimate partner.

Carroll said she was in an abusive relationship for over a decade and during that time, she convinced herself that everything was OK because she was trying to hold herself together. However, once the relationship was over in 2013, Carroll said she had to depend on God for everything in the form of protection, financial stability, and overall peace.

According to a report by the Domestic Violence Intervention Program, an organization that provides comprehensive support and advocacy services to domestic abuse victims and survivors, women are 70 times more likely to be killed in the two weeks after leaving an abusive relationship than at any other time during the relationship.

"Through all of that, God brought us (Carroll and her two sons) through the darkest, hardest, most uncomfortable place," Carroll said. "As a mother, I felt hopeless and helpless because I was supposed to take care of my children, and I felt that I couldn't. It wasn't until I decided to depend completely on Him and it wasn't until I decided that I didn't have to do anything other than stand on God's word that says I'm the head, not the tail."

When I started concentrating on His word, and completely trusting Christ, that's when the healing began...

Carroll noted that the physical scars from abuse eventually went away, but added that through her faith in Christ, God began to heal her from the inside-out.

"He literally delivered my children and me," Carroll said. "He provided, and He continues to provide. Now, years later, we are stable, and we're safe, and God has even dealt with me on the forgiveness side of the abuse."

Because I completely trusted God, He meets needs in ways that I can never understand...

Carroll stressed that she is a living testimony to anyone who has ever been in an abusive relationship and also a testimony for those who may one day find themselves in an abusive relationship.

"Psalms 139 says that I'm fearfully and wonderfully made; that's something I didn't know at the time," Carroll said. "But now I know that I don't have to hide behind cancer, something that I was diagnosed with and overcame. I don't have to hide behind abuse, and it's not fair for me to hold it, because there are other women out there going through the same thing, the same type of shame, the same type of abuse, the same type of worry about how they're going to make it. How dare I not say thank you, God, by letting other people know how He helped us and how He continues to help me, and how He continues to deliver and protect me. My testimony is that I'm a survivor of domestic violence and my goal in life is to let other survivors in the making, not victims, but survivors in the making, let them know that God is real."

GOD SAVED ME FROM DECADES OF LOOKING FOR LOVE IN THE WRONG PLACES

DARIAN HARRIS

Indian Land, South Carolina

Ever since Darian Harris was a teenager, being accepted and feeling like she was loved by the men she dated and people, in general, is something she often struggled with. But she says it wasn't until she accepted the love of Christ that she was able to see herself as the beautiful person in which God created her to be.

"When I was a teenager, I really felt like I wasn't getting the love from anybody," Harris said. "As I got older, I realized that I was depending on people, especially when it came to relationships. I was constantly on a hunt. It became a hunt to where the people I chose to be in my life were becoming worse and worse. Here's my story: I was doing well on my job and career, the things that people saw on the outside. However, privately, my life was a wreck, especially with relationships."

She had been married four times.

It was like I was determined to get this relationship thing right and I couldn't...

Eventually, the unhealthy relationships in which she allowed into her life started to affect her job performance as a call center supervisor for Sprint.

"Before I knew it, my body started failing me," Harris recalled. "I fell into a deep depression and ended up going out on disability. My arthritis kicked in to where I couldn't straighten up my limbs. I couldn't think straight. I couldn't sleep well. Everything was just crashing down on me. I started seeing a psychiatrist, a counselor, a therapist, and group therapy. I was doing all of these things, but things weren't smoothing out for me."

But that's not all. Harris said her inability to find the love that she so desperately wanted continued to affect her life to where she started smoking, drinking, and doing drugs.

"The combination of the depression, the physical illnesses, and the drugs on top of that, I was just doomed to crash at some point," Harris stressed, before adding, "At the same time, I had a two-story home in a very nice neighborhood, and no one told me that since I was on disability, my disability pay was going to drop to 60 percent of my salary, so money started becoming an issue. I just kept trying to fight my way through. Years had gone by, but I was staying afloat some kind of way. The Lord would always not let me crash all the way. It was like I was here for some purpose, and for that purpose, He was going to keep me here. It's like I always had a guardian angel going back to when I was a teenager because I had even tried to take my life a couple of times. I was even diagnosed with a borderline personality disorder. I took things very personally. I needed people to praise me, and if you said the wrong thing, it would take me in a whirl spin. I was just going through it mentally, physically, and financially. I even filed for bankruptcy during this time."

Harris said that after years of looking for love in the wrong places, she decided to step out on faith and place her life completely in God's hands.

"I asked God for a clean slate," Harris said. "I just decided to trust Him, to be content with my life, and now I know what true happiness is. I owe it all to Him. God never let me fall. There were days where I cried my eyes out, but through Him, I was able to bear it all. Today, I can say that I know that God is real. He pulled me through everything that I went through. The Lord was with me. God gave me a clean slate, and He can give anyone else a clean slate too."

CHAPTER 13
SINGLE PARENT

THROUGH FAITH IN CHRIST, I WAS ABLE TO OVERCOME A UNEXPECTED OBSTACLE IN MY LIFE

TAWANNA MCINNIS

Sugar La

Tawanna McInnis-Cole has always had high hopes for her life. She accepted Christ as her Lord and Savior at an early age. She treated people the way she wanted to be treated, just as the Golden Rule says. Academically, she excelled at K-12 and ultimately had full tuition coverage at Alcorn State University in Mississippi. Everything seemed to be going in the perfect direction, just as she had dreamed it would. But in 1998, an unexpected obstacle presented itself that, in her mind, put all of the hopes and dreams she had for herself in doubt.

"My senior year in college, I ended up pregnant," McInnis-Cole said. "This was definitely not what I had desired for myself, not what I had desired for my life. That, to me, was a tragedy. This may not be tragic to some people, but for the path that I had set for my life, it wasn't the path that I wanted it to go."

McInnis-Cole had the goal of becoming a medical doctor.

"However, this equation added to my life made me think otherwise," McInnis-Cole said. "Making wise decisions is something I had to learn to do. No longer was it all about what's best for Tawanna. It's all about what's best for Tawanna and this person that she now has to care for. Do I get a job? Do I continue forward with my dreams? How do I care for this human being that I had not planned for? How do I walk around on campus where there is a stigma? The stigma of people saying she's not married, she has no husband, but she is walking around presumably the Miss Goody-two-shoes. The one who did everything right and now look at her."

How do I walk around with my head held high with that stigma around me?

McInnis-Cole said she and her mother would always pray to keep her encouraged. But there was a moment in which McInnis-Cole says she will never forget, when her daughter was just a few days old in January 1999. McInnis-Cole and her mother were bathing her newborn baby.

"At that moment is when I felt my spirit so heavy, so desolate," McInnis-Cole recalled. "I asked myself, why did this happen to me? What am I going to do?"

I cried, and I cried, and I cried...

"I was on the floor, so upset, so torn. I couldn't say anything," McInnis-Cole recalled, before adding that's when God stepped in through a song and reminded her that she could start again, that what she was going through was not the end, and that everybody makes mistakes—even Christians.

"Life throws you challenges," McInnis-Cole said. "What you have planned may not be what God has for you, but you have to allow Him to work His will into your life and know that His will is what's best."

McInnis-Cole stressed that she had to surrender her will and let God lead her because it was clear to her that what she had planned for her life was not what God had planned.

"I had a beautiful daughter, and I was determined that she would be great," McInnis-Cole said. "I did not become a physician, but I have excelled in the medical field, and I am just as proud of myself for accomplishing that goal. But after surrendering my will to God, He guided me into a different field in medicine, and I am completely and solely satisfied with that."

McInnis-Cole's daughter is a young adult now and is academically and athletically inclined.

"I don't attribute any of her success to me; I credit it to surrendering her over to God in the first few days of her life," McInnis-Cole said. "I allowed God to move into my heart completely and give my will completely to Him and say to Him; you have to guide me to help me guide her. This is not what we had planned, but I know that your will is much better than mine. It is not what I had planned, but it has been the best thing that has ever happened to me. God saw what I needed at that moment. He saw what my parents needed at that time. He saw what my entire family needed at that time. And although initially, I viewed it as a tragedy, it was an overall blessing to me at that age, to my family, to my brother who is five years younger than me. It gave him a little bit more purpose because he was becoming an uncle and would soon have his own daughter and children to care for."

By placing my faith and life in God's hands...

McInnis-Cole completed her bachelor's degree and completed two additional degrees after having her daughter. Today, she is the Director of Infection Prevention within a 14-hospital system of one of the top hospitals in the United States. She holds a Master of Science degree, a Bachelor of Science and a nursing degree. She is a registered nurse and has a national board certification in infection control.

I BECAME A SINGLE PARENT AT AGE 17, BUT THROUGH FAITH, I WAS ABLE TO LET GO & LET GOD

MARTINE COLLEY
Virginia Beach, Virginia

Being married with children is how Martine Colley had always pictured her life, but when she gave birth to her son at age 17 in 2001, making ends meet as a single parent took on a life of its own.

"This was a time where I had to rely on no one but God, nothing but my faith brought me through it," Colley recalled. "I became pregnant at the age of 17. I had two sets of parents growing up, so for me, it was tough just accepting the idea that my son would not have the same structure of two-parents who was married with a family like I had growing up."

There was a time where I worked three jobs while attending school at the same time…

"I felt like the only way to provide for my son was with a formal education, but when I was in school, I found myself not being able to focus or concentrate because the demands of being a mother far exceeded me sitting in a classroom," Colley stressed, before adding, "I did poorly to where I had to drop out of school. As my son got older, I attempted to go back to school part-time, but my mind just wasn't there. I felt like school wasn't really providing what I needed to provide for the both of us in our immediate situation. I was working jobs that weren't career based or long-term jobs."

It was really tough for me; I felt like God was punishing me; I often asked God what did I do so wrong to deserve this situation in my life?

Colley noted that she and her son encountered many hardships through the years, but added that turning to the church and placing her life in God's hands is the best thing she could have ever done for herself and her son.

"I felt like God was able to talk with me," Colley said. "The ages 13 to 14 for my son were really tough with him just trying to connect the dots of his life."

Colley said that through prayer, God allowed her to gain understanding and to no longer have bitterness toward her circumstances as a single parent.

"I had to learn to let it go," she said. "I held on to how I felt for almost 15 years. I learned as a Christian that you have to be able to let go of thoughts of anger. Even though you may not act on it, just letting go is what you must do. Until you actually deal with it, through faith, your problems just don't go away."

Colley said she's a living testimony to all single parents that when you place your faith in God, He will answer and provide blessings and peace that surpasses all understanding.

"By placing my faith in God, I have been able to make it through all of the tough times as a single parent through the years. By trusting God, He has blessed my son and me with good times," Colley said.

Today, Colley has a successful career in corporate administration and is a licensed real estate agent.

CHAPTER 14
MARRIAGE & DIVORCE

I NEVER THOUGHT I WOULD MARRY AGAIN, BUT GOD BLESSED ME WITH A WONDERFUL HUSBAND

MICHELLE FAU

Auste

Divorced, hurt, and spiritually and emotionally wounded, Michelle Faulkner, some 14 years ago doubted that she would ever find her knight in shining armor. She wished, hoped, and prayed for God to send her a loving husband in which she could spend the rest of her life. Today, she credits her faith in God as the reason why her wish came true.

"I can honestly say that God has answered my prayers," she said. "Words can't describe my journey."

The journey she speaks of is the journey that many women also say they want: to be married to their soulmate. But a painful divorce in 1993 after three years of marriage left Faulkner emotionally scared to the point to where she didn't know if she would ever find the love of her life.

"It was rough," Faulkner recalled. "I prayed for God to bring me a good man, a man who could be my husband, a man who would love me, love my child, and grow old with me."

Today, she credits her faith in Jesus Christ for the life she has today: happily married with children she shares with her husband, Derrick.

God shows up when you least expect Him to...

It was, as Michelle describes, a Divine connection in which she and her husband Derrick ended up going out on a date. It was the week before Christmas, December 17, 2006, in which her now mother-in-law, asked her if she wanted to see the sneak preview of the movie Dream Girls featuring Beyoncé Knowles and Jennifer Hudson.

"She said she had two tickets and her son, Derrick, from Atlanta, was in town visiting Fort Lauderdale, where I lived at the time," Faulkner said. "We went to the movies, and from that point on, I knew I had found something special. You could feel something in the room. In fact, less than two years later, in 2008, we married in Las Vegas."

Faulkner said she's living proof that there is somebody out there for everybody.

"I now have my dream guy," Faulkner said, before adding, "My message to those still searching, hoping and praying for God to send them their soulmate, is to simply place your faith in God and He will bring you your knight in shining armor. What He did for me, He will do for you too."

I BECAME DIVORCED AFTER
32 YEARS OF MARRIAGE,
BUT BY PLACING MY FAITH
IN CHRIST, I'M MORE BLESSED
THAN I'VE EVER BEEN

Patricia Wiggin was always taught in the church that once you get married, you stay married until death does you part, so when she and her husband divorced in 2011 after 32 years of marriage, she had no idea that God was setting her up for one of the biggest blessings of her life.

"I had been married for 32 years, so I ended up having to start my life all over again," Wiggin said. "I got married at age 19. Now here I was 51 years old and scared absolutely to death because this is all I had known for 32 years. However, a year and a half before that, there was a person on my job who was going through a divorce. I kept being her cheerleader and telling her that if God sees you to it, He's going to see you through it. I was talking the talk in her situation, but now I had to walk the walk in my own situation."

I had never fully read the Bible until that time in my life...

"I started in the New Testament and then went to the Old Testament," Wiggin said. "There were a lot of things in there that rang true, that made me stronger coming through to the other side of my divorce," Wiggin recalled. "It was absolutely the scariest point in my entire life. I'm a witness that even during the worst or scariest time in your life that by placing your faith in God, He will restore you. I found strength in scripture, the church, and in Christ."

God blessed Wiggin to remarry in 2013. Her husband's name is Buddy.

"I stepped out on faith in Christ, and He rewarded me with a great husband," Wiggin said. "I have been restored, and I am happier than I've ever been in my life."

GOD BLESSED ME WITH A
GOD-FEARING HUSBAND

When Brenda Sheridan lost her husband to cancer on April 26, 2003, she thought that she would spend the rest of her life alone. But with a renewed focus on Jesus Christ as her Lord and Savior, Sheridan says her faith was not only strengthened, but God also blessed her with a new husband.

"This is God's business," Sheridan said. "I lost my husband to cancer, a rare form of cancer that attacks the bone but is not bone cancer. The entire time we were married, I looked to my husband for everything. He took care of everything. He was a deacon in the church, and I looked more to him than I did God. I know that wasn't a good thing, but I depended upon him for a lot of things. I guess I had taken my focus off of God at the time. Once he got sick, he was sick for three to four years, and it was totally unexpected. I asked God, why me?"

Sheridan recalled that the days, months, and years following her husband's death, were extremely hard; even enduring times where she felt that some family members turn their backs on her.

"I had some family members tell me, Brenda; you knew he was sick, why were you all traveling so much? But in my mind I was saying, that's what he wanted to do, so that's what we did," Sheridan said.

I refocused on God...

"I completely shut myself off, I said God, use me in any way you can, and at that time, I had a closer walk with God," Sheridan stressed, before adding that she didn't want to be alone, so she decided to renew her focus, trust, and faith in the Lord.

"God, in His Word, said that man is never meant to be alone, so He gave Adam a helpmate," Sheridan declared. "This is how God worked it out for me: I placed my faith in God and left it in His hands. So one day I went back home, and I happen to meet up with an old classmate in which I had known of for over 50 years, and God said, that's the one."

> *I had been single for 12 years, and he had been single for 12 years, and we just connected, and the rest was history...*

"I thank God that God saw fit to place someone else in my life because He knew that I had gone through a lot," said Sheridan, who married her husband, Ben Sheridan, in 2015.

"To this day, I never would have imagined that I would have somebody else in my life," Sheridan stressed. "I thank God for doing that for me, because I know it was nobody but Him. I want to say to anybody who feels like giving up, don't give up. We don't know the plans that God has for us. He will never leave us, and He will never forsake us, and we have to remember that God loves us. He loves us more than we love ourselves. My husband is a God-fearing man, and we're walking this journey together. I didn't want to be unequally yoked. I wanted a God-fearing man. I thank God for sending him my way."

I STEPPED OUT ON FAITH TO MARRY MY HUSBAND

WANDA LISTER

Fort Mill, South Carolina

When Wanda Lister was a little girl, she daydreamed about who she would marry and spend the rest of her life with. But she says she would have never experienced the life she has today with her soulmate if she didn't step out on faith to marry her husband.

"I was told that he was not the one for me," Lister recalled. "I was a member of this particular church for five years, and the minister at the church told me that the person I wanted to marry was unequally yoked with me. But I had prayed for God send me a husband because I had three children and no father figure who was present for them."

I felt that God had sent me a husband, and the pastor said, no...

Lister said she had three children from previous marriages, but noted, that she decided that the next marriage would work out the way it should.

"I went out on faith to do everything God's way," Lister said. "I was doing everything, abstaining from sex, doing everything that I felt I needed to do in order for God to give me my wish of having a husband, but when we were sitting in the pastor's office talking, the pastor said, no, I'm not going to marry you."

I was very hurt because I had asked God for a mate...

Lister says she was hurt because she had high regard for church pastors and felt that she needed her pastor's blessing in order to marry.

"I prayed about it, and I got married," Lister said, before adding, "we've been together married for over 30 years and my husband, Oscar, who served 21 years in the United States Army, has been a wonderful father to my three children. My testimony to others who may be facing a similar situation, where your friends, family, and even a pastor are against it. If you feel that you're doing what God tells you to do, that's what you need to go by, not by what man says you should do, or who you should marry. Everybody may not be in agreement with who you marry, but by faith in Christ, God can and will bring you the right person for you at the right time. I'm a living witness to what faith in God can do."

CHAPTER 15
FAMILY & CHILDBIRTH

"THE DOCTOR SAID I WOULDN'T HAVE ANOTHER CHILD, BUT I'VE HAD 12 CHILDREN

BARBARA JO WROTEN PAYNE
Moss Point, Mississippi

I n 1955, **Barbara Jo Wroten Payne was told by doctors that** she would not have another child due to the complications she experienced during the birth of her first child. However, she says her faith in Christ proved to be the driving force for her to not only have another child, but to have a total of 12 children, 21 grandchildren, and 34 great-grandchildren.

"This story is the very first encounter on how God worked in my life," Payne said. "When I had my first child, I went into convulsion. My baby was a day old before I knew my baby was born. Everybody told me that I wouldn't have another baby, and even the doctors said that I would not have another baby."

I placed my trust in God's hands...

"I became pregnant again, and the entire nine months of my pregnancy, everyone was asking, aren't you afraid? But for some reason I was peaceful inside," Payne said. "I knew the danger that I had gone through during my first pregnancy, but I still had peace. And when the time had come in which my baby was due, the doctors said that there was no sign of labor. Finally, one Friday when I had my doctor's appointment, he said, if you don't go into labor by Sunday, we're going to put you into the hospital and induce labor."

Payne said she went home that day and told her husband, Robert Payne Sr., what the doctor said. Her husband then asked her if she had spoken to her mother about her pregnancy.

"I said I did, and my mother told me that when the time comes, the baby will come," Payne recalled, before adding, "My husband told me, 'well, the doctor has never had a baby, you listen to your mom.'"

So that night when I went to bed, I got on my knees, and I asked the Lord: show me what to do...

"In my mind, I knew my doctor knew what he was talking about and I knew my mother knew what she was talking about also," Payne stressed. "So I just prayed and asked the Lord to show me, and that morning before day, I woke up with a little twinge in my back. I went to the bathroom, and there was a sign that it was time for birth, meaning I had the symptoms. I had the signs of labor, so I had no fear when it was time for me to go to the hospital that Sunday evening. I gave birth to a beautiful boy, and I knew that the Lord did it in response to my faith in Him to allow me to have another child even though the doctor told me years before that I would never give birth to another child."

Payne said she always shares this story of how God allowed her to have another child because it glorifies God and gives hope to others who have also been told that it's impossible for them to give birth.

"I heard a preacher say once that we're all blessed when we're up and out, but when you're highly favored, is when the Lord does something special specifically for you and you know He did it for you," Payne said. "I felt like I was really highly favored at that time for my child's birth. After that, I had 10 more babies, and now I am a great, great grandmother, and I'm so thankful, because I know I'm highly favored. It's all because of faith in Jesus Christ."

I COULDN'T CONCEIVE, BUT ONCE I PUT MY FAITH IN ONLY GOD, HE BLESSED ME WITH THREE SONS

CYNTHIA COLE
Holly Springs, Mississippi

C ynthia Cole was 24 years old when she and her husband married in October 1971. Young, vibrant, and excited to start a family, Cole and her husband started trying to have a child. But nothing happened. For years—five years to be exact, the couple tried to have a child. They tried medical treatments and various other procedures. Still, nothing happened.

"One Christmas I was speaking with an older lady in the community, and she said perhaps we were trying too hard and she recommended that we read the Bible, a particular story and to pray a particular prayer," Cole recalled.

I read Hannah's prayer for a son...

The story of Hannah is found in 1 Samuel, chapters 1 and 2. Hannah, according to the biblical story, was loved by her husband, Elkanah, but the Lord had closed her womb. Being childless, she vowed to God that if He gave her a son, she would give him to the Lord all the days of his life. After some time had passed, God answered Hannah's prayer, and she conceived and had a son. Because she had asked for him from the Lord, she named him Samuel, which means "asked or heard of God." Hannah kept her word as she had vowed. After Samuel was weaned, she presented him to Eli, the priest.

"Hannah was barren, and I read that verse, and I did pray," Cole stressed. "I was sincerely praying, just like Hannah."

Within three months I was pregnant with our first child...

"If it had not been for faith and the grace of God, I don't know if I would have my three sons that I have today," Cole said, before adding that she often laughs when she thinks back on her prayer, saying that God took her literally, because she and her husband only had sons and Hannah's prayer was for a son.

"That's my testimony, because of God and through my faith in Christ, God's mercy and through God's grace, I have three wonderful sons that I wouldn't take anything for," Cole said. "We had tried to have children for a lot of years and did a lot of medical procedures and methods, but none of them worked, so I attribute my sons to faith in Christ and His grace."

"
BY TRUSTING GOD,
I WENT FROM LIVING IN A
ONE-BEDROOM APARTMENT
TO HAVING A FOUR-BEDROOM
HOME & A FAMILY

DERRICK J. FAULKNER
Atlanta, Georgia

Proverbs 18:22 declares that he who finds a wife finds a good thing and obtains the favor of the Lord. Derrick J. Falkner says trusting Christ is what led him to find his wife, his good thing, who helped him turn his entire life around.

"Growing up, I had an up and down journey as a Christian," Faulkner said, before adding, "I felt like I let God down with the lifestyle I was living. I spent time in jail. I became divorced because I was unfaithful to my first wife. But I'm thankful that God gave me the whooping that I needed. I got to a point in my life to where I didn't see the value of my life. I was not suicidal, but I was really looking for that purpose. I was fortunate enough to be able to start anew."

An old man once told me that to get something you've never had before; you have to do something you've never done before...

Faulkner was raised in the church and was baptized as a youth, but just as others can relate to, he found himself straying away from how he was raised and the teachings of the Bible. He decided to make a change, to step out on faith, and put his life in God's hands.

I said, God, if you bless me with a wife, this time I will stay faithful...

"Little did I know that I would soon propose to my wife, Michelle, a woman who would help change my life," Faulkner stressed. "This is how you know God's Word is real. When I married Michelle, I was hustling for a living. I was working a couple of part-time jobs. I was a DJ; I was selling mixtapes and CDs. I thought I was doing pretty good. I was living in a one-bedroom apartment. I wasn't making a lot of money, but I was doing decent."

But I wanted better, so I decided to trust God to receive better, God's favor...

When Faulkner and his wife, Michelle married in 2008, they moved into a two-bedroom apartment. Faulkner said he kept reminding himself of the promise he made to God and what Proverbs 18:22 said, that he had God's favor, now that he had a wife, his good thing. He waited on God and trusted that God's favor would eventually manifest itself in his life.

"One of the guys I used to sell CDs to offered me a job driving at Follett Corporation, a company that provides a variety of educational products to schools, but little did I know that that driving job would prosper into where I am today," Faulkner said. "I started off as a part-time driver, driving a couple of days a week. They admired my leadership, and they offered me a management position. Within a couple of years, that management position turned into a project management position."

My life just really took off from there...

"Before I knew it, we were leaving the two bedroom apartment to moving into a four bedroom, two-story home," Faulkner revealed. "I can't begin to tell you how when you stay faithful to not only God but to your marriage, the blessings that come from that. I'm talking about vehicles, surprise checks in the mail, numerous blessings that comes from finding a wife, that good thing."

Faulkner said that he is a walking, living, and breathing testimony, that by putting your faith in Jesus Christ, anybody can go from having nothing to having something, despite whatever happened in their past.

"When you trust Him, He will bless you," Faulkner said. "I know this because He did it for me."

THROUGH FAITH, GOD
BLESSED OUR BLENDED FAMILY

ANITA WALTON MOORE
Holly Springs, Mississippi

W hen Anita Moore and her husband, Arvern Moore married, they always wanted to have two children, a boy, and a girl, in that order. God blessed them with just that. But a family tragedy during the summer of 1971 changed all the plans they had set for their family, and Moore says it was only their faith in Christ that brought them through it.

"We were vacationing in Hot Springs, Arkansas when we got the news that my husband, Arvern Moore, sister, Janice had been killed in a car accident, leaving behind eight children, four boys, and four girls," Moore said. "Janice's ailing mother was the beneficiary of the children ranging from ages three to 17. This devastating news left us in a wondering state of mind asking ourselves, 'what are we going to do?' There was no way their ailing mother could afford to take care of eight additional people in her home. However, she tried for several years, but the oldest daughter started to rebel and ended up in jail. I took the oldest daughter into our home in 1976, and several years later, I took the other three girls."

I asked the questions: Why am I responsible for children that are not my blood kin? Why is God putting this financial burden on us?

Moore said after much prayer, she decided to place her faith in God's hands to be able to support the additional members of their family financially.

"It took a while, but all the pieces to the puzzle fell into place," Moore revealed. "Our two biological children accepted their cousins with open arms, and we were very happy to have a house full, going from having two children to having a total of six."

Years later,

two of our children went off to college, which made our financial obligations more difficult...

"All we could do is keep praying to God," Moore recalled, before adding, "God kept giving us answers. Through all the ups and downs we suffered, God made a way out of no way. Through faith in God, we never missed a meal, and all of our bills were paid. In fact, we always seemed to have more than most people had. Our story of faith is a testament to what God can do if you trust Him when unexpected circumstances arrive in your life."

All four girls (Normie, Brenda, Chloe, and Cherrie), Moore said, are doing very well in life and reside in the Atlanta Metro area.

"I WAS TOLD THAT I WOULD NEVER BE ABLE TO HAVE CHILDREN, BUT WITH GOD, I'VE GIVEN BIRTH TO THREE CHILDREN

BETTY JEAN KING
Fayetteville, Georgia

When Betty Jean King was a junior in college at Bethune-Cookman University in 1981, she had one of the worst experiences a woman could experience—she was raped.

"I was 20 years old at the time," King recalled. "From that, I later discovered that I was pregnant."

The child, however, was never born, and due to complications related to the pregnancy, King was told by doctors that she would never be able to have children again. But King credits this time in her life to having a closer walk with God and getting to know intimately who God is and that by faith and trust in God, all things are possible.

"At the time I didn't know God as I know Him now," King said. "In 1984, I joined a church in Atlanta and surrounded myself with a strong group of God-fearing women. From there, my faith in God grew. I wanted to have children, although I was told that I would never be able to any more children."

But God's word says otherwise...

King said her faith was strengthened after reading Deuteronomy 7:13-14, which says, 'And He will love you and bless you and multiply you; He will also bless the fruit of your womb and the fruit of your land, your grain and your new wine and your oil, the increase of your cattle and the offspring of your flock, in the land of which He swore to your fathers to give you. You shall be blessed above all peoples; there shall not be a male or female barren among you or among your livestock.' "This is one of the scriptures in the Bible that let me know that by trusting God at His word, that having children, for me, was very much so possible. I prayed, and I prayed and through faith in God, I got married in 1990.'"

On October 17, 1991, my son was born...

"God not only blessed me to have one child, but I also gave birth to two more children after that, so I have three children, Isaac, Gabriel, and Christina," King said, before adding, "I am a living testimony at what God can do once you put your faith in Him. I was told that I would never be able to have children, but God blessed me with three children, one for the Father, one for the Son, and one for the Holy Spirit. I just want to encourage someone out there who wants to have children or have been told that there is no way for it happen. I'm living proof that by putting your faith in Christ, it's possible."

BY FAITH, GOD SAVED MY FIRSTBORN SON

MARVIA E. KILGORE
Byhalia, Mississippi

October 24, 1972, is a day that Marvia Kilgore will never forget. It was the day that she gave birth to her first child, Sylvester Kilgore Jr. But it was also the day in which she says her faith in God was tested like it had never been tested before.

Her newborn son was diagnosed with a condition in which only 1 in 10,000 to 15,000 newborns in the United States develop, a condition called Phenylketonuria, commonly known as PKU.

"I was 23 years old, and I gave birth to my son on that day," Kilgore said, before adding that what happened next was something she did not expect, a problem in which only God could fix.

"The doctor came into my hospital room with the nurses, and they were looking at my child, examining him and asking me a lot of questions, so a level of anxiety came over me," Kilgore recalled. "Nothing was said to me at that time, but the next day, which was the third day after Sylvester Jr.'s birth, they came in, and they started talking about giving him a blood test. They pricked his heel, and later on that night they came back and told us that he had a blood disorder. They were saying that's why he was sort of yellowish in color. They said he was jaundice. They said that it was something that was serious, but it could be treated.

They proceeded to tell us that the name of this disorder, they call it PKU for short, but it has a long scientific name (Phenylketonuria). Really what it amounted to is that it is a genetic disorder that could not process the amino acids in his blood. They went on to tell us that if left untreated that it would cause mental retardation, learning disability, seizures, just a whole host of problems."

They told us that the treatment was a blood transfusion...

"With this being my first time having a baby and hearing this news, you can imagine my anxiety was very high, but that afternoon we consented for him to have the blood transfusion," Kilgore explained. "They took us away to Le Bonheur Children's Hospital in Memphis."

They took all of his blood out and put new blood in...

"We just prayed all during the time, because it was just so overwhelming, asking God to save our child, that our child would be healthy and well," Kilgore recalled. "In the end, we said, let your will be done, and we had faith that God was going to see us through, that the success of this blood transfusion was going to make Sylvester Jr. healthy."

Kilgore noted that she stayed at Le Bonheur Children's Hospital in Memphis for two days after the operation while doctors observed him to ensure that there were not any complications.

"Slowly his color started to change, and he was discharged being free of the PKU," Kilgore said. "During that trying time, I put my faith in God, and I felt like it was going to be alright, and it was. It was out of my hands, and all I could do is place my faith in Christ. I have tried to live a life of faith because I believe what the Bible says, and I try to practice that. I believe He got us through that particular situation and many other things, and I believe that He will continue to make a way out of no way for my family. We didn't know what was going to happen. God saved my son. What He did for us, He is able to do for someone else through faith. That's my testimony."

Today, Kilgore's son, Sylvester Jr., is the Athletic Director at Holly Springs High School, located in Holly Springs, Mississippi.

GOD TOOK CARE OF MY FAMILY WHEN I COULDN'T

BEN COLE III

Soso, Mississippi

Ben Cole III was 26 years old when he found himself in a powerful position of leadership as the General Manager of the Holiday Inn in Hattiesburg, Mississippi, but he had no power when it came to protecting his family for one of the worst natural disasters the United States has ever seen: Hurricane Katrina.

"The situation was Hurricane Katrina. I had a hotel full of guests, and I had to trust in God to be able to lead and keep families calm under the situation," Cole recalled.

I had no communication with my family for three days once Hurricane Katrina hit

At about 6 a.m., August 29, 2005, Hurricane Katrina made landfall as a Category 3 storm with 127 miles per hour winds between Grand Isle, Louisiana, and the mouth of the Mississippi River. Hurricane Katrina killed 238 people in Mississippi and 1,577 in New Orleans, directly or indirectly, according to the Federal Emergency Management Agency. Two died in Alabama, 14 in Florida and two in Georgia, for a total of 1,833 souls lost.

The 27-foot storm surge washed away thousands of homes and businesses along the Mississippi Gulf Coast and up to 18 inches of rain in some areas. According to FEMA, the total damage for Katrina is estimated at $108 billion, making it one of the costliest hurricanes in US history.

"I didn't know if they were OK, I had no way to reach them, so all I could do is put my faith and trust in God to protect them and keep them safe," said Cole. "I had a three-month-old child, my firstborn child, and I didn't know if my wife and daughter were OK, or whether they were stranded or in distress."

According to the *Hattiesburg American Newspaper*, thousands of evacuees from Mississippi, Alabama, and Louisiana clogged U.S. 49, U.S. 98 and Interstate 59, where Cole was located at the Holiday Inn in Hattiesburg, Mississippi. In fact, the city of Hattiesburg, the city in which Cole was working as a hotel manager, ran out of motel rooms; within hours. The closest room to be found was in Memphis, a five-hour drive north of Hattiesburg.

"I was finally able to make it 30 miles to my home in Soso, Mississippi, to see that they were all safe and the structure of our house was unharmed," Cole said. "I had to believe in God and trust in Him."

During the time that I was unable to communicate with my family, I was reminded of having the patience of Job in the Bible...

"Thoughts like that, to be patient like Job in the Bible, went through my head and also being able to control my emotions being a 20-something-year-old male in that leadership role," Cole reflected. "I think that lesson in having faith in Christ and patience has stayed with me. It has made me a better person, a better leader, and stronger in my faith in God."

CHAPTER 16
MISTAKES

"

GOD GAVE ME ANOTHER CHANCE AFTER I MADE A BIG MISTAKE

TASHA GRANT
Houston, Texas

We all make mistakes, but when the Houston Independent School District (HISD)—one of the nation's largest school district's—announced an investigation of suspicious results on 2004 statewide tests, Tasha Grant's career and life as she knew it was put in jeopardy due to a mistake she made. However, she credits her faith in God for giving her another chance.

"In the year 2003-2004, I was a fifth-grade teacher in HISD," Grant said. "It was my first year of teaching, and I had never been exposed to the ins and outs of teaching. During testing, we are under very tight security to prevent any kind of testing irregularities, but the school I was teaching at, the culture was to assist students with state testing. I was influenced into doing so, and I did. I knew it was wrong, and the state eventually found out about it."

I could have possibly gone to jail and had my certifications revoked...

As a result, Grant and one other teacher were removed from their classrooms and placed in HISD's district building for a month and a half while an investigation ensued.

"During that month, we were being questioned, we had several depositions taken, and they were questioning the students on whether we were helping them," Grant recalled.

This was on the local news, but our names were never shared, so nobody knew who we were...

"The district lawyers were questioning us; they were questioning the children, the principals and the counselors," Grant recalled. "I knew I was wrong because I did something bad. I was very remorseful, and I prayed, and I prayed when I sat out that whole month. I had long periods of time to talk to God while I was waiting."

Grant added that although the general public didn't know her name, or that she was involved in the state test score incident, she is sharing her testimony now because she wants others to know that everyone makes mistakes and bad choices—even Christians.

"I was young, I made a mistake, and the only thing that I could do is put my faith and trust in God," Grant said, before adding, "In the end, all of the charges were dismissed."

The blessing in it all, according to Grant, is that God gave her another chance to move on from her mistake.

"God blessed me with a new job in a new district without even having to go through the interview process," Grant said. "I was hired the same day I interviewed. My testimony is that since my mistake, I have been awarded Teacher of The Year three times, so you can't tell me that God is not good. I am a living testimony that God still loves you even when you make a mistake and that He is faithful when you put your trust and faith in Him to bring you through whatever it is you're going through."

"I WENT TO PRISON, BUT GOD GAVE ME ANOTHER CHANCE

LAMONT PAYNE
Brooklyn, New York

I n the 1980s, Lamont Payne was heavy into drugs. He distributed and sold them, something that he learned early in life from watching his father sell drugs. But when his dealings landed him in prison, Payne says the only thing that he could do is trust that God would give him another chance at living a normal life once he left prison.

"At a young age I went to school with a lot of drugs in my pocket," Payne recalled. "I reaped the benefits of my dad doing drugs. I had a lot of drugs on me that kids were very attracted to."

But those same drugs caused his life to come to a standstill. It led to prison time.

"I chose the life in which I thought was a good life, but it wasn't the life that God had for me," Payne stressed, before adding, "I had to go through my go through because what I did back then made me who I am today. I thank God that I had to go that rough way."

Payne said there's a common question in the mind of most people serving time behind bars. That question is wondering how they will be accepted by society once they leave prison and whether they will have the ability to get a job without their past coming back to haunt them.

I decided to put my faith in God to open doors for me, doors that I could not open on my own...

While in prison, Payne put his faith into action by preparing himself for whatever doors God would open for him once he was released from prison. His faith in God led him to live in prison as if he was already on the outside, looking to secure opportunities.

I got my GED in prison, I went to college in prison, and I married my wife in prison...

"I am not ashamed of that, because what God brought me through, I am a testimony for someone who is down and out," Payne said, before noting that the result of his faith in Christ is, "Today I am working with some of the best doctors in the nation at Methodist Hospital. I have a good job, and God is using my life as a testimony. With my story of faith, I am trying to free someone that's in captivity and can't see no way out. I truly believe that God is a second chance God. I am a Christian who received another chance. Through faith, God can turn everything around."

Payne, who is also now a licensed minister of the Gospel, stressed that Psalms 124:2-5 is a scripture in which he keeps near and dear to his heart.

"If it had not been for the Lord, who is on my side, where would I be? That's all I hold on to," Payne declared. "That's my scripture that I hold on to because I truly believe in that. I should have been dead and gone, but we serve a God of another chance. I just want to let anyone who has ever gone to prison or has made some wrong choices in life know that when you go on faith, trust and believe that God—Jesus Christ, can give you a clean slate and give you another chance at life. I'm a living witness that He will do it. All you have to do is trust Him, and He will show up."

"MY MISTAKE LANDED ME IN FEDERAL PRISON AT AGE 71, BUT IT WAS THE BEST THING THAT COULD HAVE EVER HAPPENED TO ME

ELLENESE BROOKS-SIMMS
New Orleans, Louisiana

E llenese Brooks-Simms says she is the perfect example of how someone who was raised in the church, was baptized at age 10, had a successful career in the Louisiana public school system for more than 40 years, can as a Christian fall victim to making choices that go against everything she stands for. But she says being sent to federal prison at the age of 71 is the best thing that could have ever happened to her because it reconnected her with Christ.

"I understand what I did and that what I did was wrong," Brooks-Simms said. "I knew it was wrong at the time. Out of what I thought was desperation, I did what I did. Most of all, I apologize to the children I taught and to the people in the community who respected me. I betrayed their trust."

Brooks-Simms was sentenced in March 2010 to 18 months in federal prison for accepting $140,000 in bribes in return for her support of an algebra software program. However, prosecutors requested the extremely lenient sentence, down from the six to seven years recommended by federal guidelines, because of her help in securing the conviction of another individual. Brooks-Simms pleaded guilty to a single count of conspiracy to defraud the federal government and alluded to financial problems that led her to take the bribes.

I'm a Christian, and I'm living proof that sometimes we as Christians make mistakes, but I want to encourage others and let them know that despite our mistakes, regardless of how bad it is, we can still go to Christ for help...

Brooks-Simms admitted that while climbing the latter of success, she lost focus, and became caught up with titles, positions, and things of the world, something that she says Satan can use to lure even seasoned Christians down the wrong path. While serving time in federal prison, Brookes-Simms says she was able to re-connect with Christ.

"All I could do is place my trust and faith in God," Brooks-Simms said. "I never thought I would be where I was. I had lived most of my life. Out of all the things I did good, all it took was the wrong choice to erase it all. If you Google me, you'll have to search really hard and deep to find all the good I did throughout my life. But I tell my testimony of making the choice I made because you never know other Christians who have also made a choice that now has them feeling a certain way. I want them to know that God still accepts them and that they can go on. Our God is a God who gives us more than one or two chances, but He is a God of another chance. When I tell people that I served time in prison, they always say—no, not you! I tell them, yes. Yes me. I did. But by faith, I am here today, and I hope that my story helps someone else who has ever done something they wish they could take back."

CHAPTER 17
RETIREMENT

I WAS AFRAID TO RETIRE, BUT BY TRUSTING GOD, A WHOLE NEW WORLD HAS OPENED UP FOR ME

IRA JOHNSON
Fort Lauderdale, Florida

According to a report from the Insured Retirement Institute, more 10,000 Baby Boomers will exit the workforce each day between now and the end of next decade, with 45 percent having absolutely no retirement savings and 59 percent relying heavily on Social Security.

Ira Johnson is one of the thousands of Baby Boomers who were facing retirement in 2011, but she says putting her faith in God, has opened up a whole new world for her.

"When I retired in 2011, I had 38 years of service with AT&T, and I had no idea how I would spend my time," Johnson recalled." I wasn't ready to retire, but they were offering a buyout. In the back of my mind, I was thinking that I'm too young to retire, because I'm still vibrant, and I didn't know what I would do. The rumor was that the office in which I was working in would close within a year and that the jobs would be eliminated anyway."

Although Johnson was afraid of what not having a job meant for her, she decided to take the severance package AT&T was offering.

"When I put in my notice, I was still skeptical," Johnson said. "They gave me a call and said my retirement had been accepted. I was scared; I wanted to back out of it. I didn't know what I would do."

For 38 years I worked for one company, many of my friends were still working, and I had to go out on faith to retire, and I believed that God would show me a way to continue doing some of the things I love to do…

Johnson describes herself as a peoples person and someone who doesn't like sitting around at home all day.

"I have to admit that I enjoyed being home for the first two or three weeks, because I didn't have to get up early to go to work, and I spent most of my time running errands that I hadn't had time to do while I was working," Johnson said.

But Johnson said God soon rewarded her for her faith in Him by showing up while she took her grandson to baseball practice at a local community center. While her grandson was at baseball practice, she noticed a bulletin board encouraging people to sign up for exercise classes.

"I decided to sign up for Zumba and yoga twice a week at a senior center," Johnson said. "Once I went there, I met a lot of people, retired school teachers. I decided to stay and have lunch. There were a lot of people there playing cards and dominos."

Being the social butterfly that Johnson is, she decided to introduce one of her favorite card games to everyone called Phase 10, a game in which the object of the game is to be the first player to complete 10 phase sequences.

"I ended up teaching a lot of people how to play Phase 10," Johnson said, before adding, "Now every day, someone comes to me wanting me to teach them how to play Phase 10. We have two tables between 10 and 12 people every day."

In addition to Johnson's love for playing card games, she is also an avid traveler and savvy with social media.

"Last year, I took a total of 10 trips, some short trips, some longer cruises to Hawaii and Caribbean cruises," Johnson said.

People were telling me how I'm always doing things and that I should teach other people how to enjoy being a retiree...

So Johnson started thinking, and before she knew it, she had started a business where she conducts seminars for seniors.

"We travel to community centers teaching them on how to enjoy life, how to get on social media and how to use a computer," Johnson explained. "I am in the process of expanding my services to corporations."

Johnson noted that unlike how most Baby Boomers grew up sharing memories with physical pictures and phone calls to family members, many of those she instructs at the senior centers have grandchildren and other family members who simply text or share their live events on Facebook, Instagram, Twitter, and other social media outlets, which is unfamiliar territory for many Baby Boomers, who feel left out because they are not participants on social media, or don't understand how social media works.

"Through social media, they are able to keep up with other people, and I'm able to help them," said Johnson. "I am so grateful that God has allowed me to have a full life in retirement doing this. When I was scared and didn't know what I would do, I stepped out on faith."

Johnson's advice to others who are facing retirement is to put their trust and faith in the Almighty God.

"Faith has worked out for me, so now I have been able to carve out a wonderful life that is truly fulfilling," Johnson said.

CHAPTER 18
COLLEGE

THE LORD MADE A WAY
OUT OF NO WAY

CALVIN CALEB

The year was 1997, and like most parents, Calvin Caleb was excited that his oldest daughter Coneka was attending college. Coneka had just finished the first semester of her junior year at Xavier University in New Orleans. Her grades were wonderful, and she was enjoying her experience as a college student. But in order for her to re-enroll for the second semester at Xavier, it would take a bold act of faith on the part of her father.

The tuition bill of $15,000 had to be paid in order for Coneka to return to school for the second semester, but her father, Calvin Caleb, didn't have the money to pay it, nor was he in a position to borrow the money from the bank, friends, or family.

"Unlike it was in the past, I did not have a job in the oil & gas industry which I had worked most of my career," Caleb recalled. "I was working at Home Depot making $9.50 an hour. It was hard just to make ends meet with my wife and family. My daughter came home after the first semester, and she was very concerned as to how we were going to pay her tuition for the winter semester. I told my daughter that we would have to trust in God, that no, I didn't have the money, but I believe that God will make a way somehow for you to continue on in school."

Caleb had a choice to make. Would he keep his daughter home because they didn't have the money to pay her college tuition, or would he put his faith in God to make a way out of no way?

At the time, Caleb was living in Houston, Texas, which is a five-hour drive to Xavier University. Caleb, with no way to pay the tuition bill, decided to pack up his truck and drive his daughter to school anyway.

All I had was $23 cash and a gas card in my pocket...

"We left Texas and headed to New Orleans, Louisiana, and on that day as I recall, all I had was $23 cash and a Chevron gas card in my pocket," Caleb said. "We packed up her footlocker, and other clothes put them on the back of my little Nissan pickup truck and headed for New Orleans."

When they arrived to register at Xavier University, the cashier quickly informed the Caleb's that $15,000 in tuition had to be paid for Coneka to attend school the second semester. Caleb informed the cashier that he didn't have the money to pay the tuition at that time. In response, the cashier then asked him what was he going to do?

"I said well, we just trusted in the Lord, and that's why we came here from Texas, believing that the Lord would make a way somehow," Caleb said. "And the whole time Coneka was standing by me hearing the whole conversation. The lady's name was Sharron. She had a large stack of paper on her desk for students who were requesting financial aid. She picked up that stack, which looked to be about two inches thick. She looked at me and said, 'Mr. Caleb, do you see this stack? This represents students who need financial aid to go to Xavier.'"

Calvin Caleb stressed to the registrar that he just didn't have the money, but insisted that his daughter needed to stay in school.

"Ms. Sharron looked down, and she started writing," Caleb recalled. "After some time had passed, she looked up and said Coneka can start this semester. I said, thank you, Jesus! My daughter Coneka was standing right there. She saw how God opened the doors of that university to allow her to continue on in school. I said Coneka, today you have witnessed how the Lord will make a way when you just trust in Him and don't doubt in your heart that he'll open doors for you."

I rejoiced driving back to Texas with $23 cash in my pocket and one gas card

A year later, Coneka graduated with a degree in child psychology. Today she has a successful career in her field of study. Caleb said he often wonders to himself what would have become of his daughter had he simply gave up and stayed home in Texas that day in 1997, because he didn't have the $15,000 to pay for the tuition.

"This is an experience that my daughter and I will never forget," Caleb said. "Whenever my daughter is in a bind, this is an event that she'll always be able to look back on, that event at Xavier University when the Lord opened up a marvelous door for her to continue on in school."

**BY TRUSTING GOD, I WAS ABLE
TO GET A COLLEGE DEGREE**

KAREN FOUNTA

Moss Point, Mississ

F or Karen Fountain, trusting and believing in God is something she learned to do at an early age, but when she became pregnant her freshman year in college in 1976, putting her faith in God that He had a plan for her life and her newborn daughter is her testimony that God can turn a difficult situation into a blessing.

"I became a teenage mother at the age of 17 in May of 1977," Fountain said. "This event began my strong prayer life. We always went to church and participated in youth programs, but my personal relationship with Christ didn't really start until I was faced with being a teenage mom."

I found myself praying hard, asking God for forgiveness and for guidance for me and my baby...

Fountain said she could not rely on her daughter's father for support.

"I asked God to help me raise her, so I would only depend on Him and the support of my parents," Fountain said, before adding that she started her first year of college, but was not able to continue her college education and provide for her at the same time. At that moment, she had a specific request for God.

I asked God to help me take care of her, to get her through college, and then I would return to college once my daughter finished...

God heard and answered Fountain's prayer.

"In 1999, prior to my daughter's graduation from college, I went back to college," Fountain said.

Romans 8:28 says, "And we know that all things work together for good to those who love God, to those who are the called according to His purpose."

Fountain had the perfect setup.

I was working for a company that participated in employee tuition reimbursement, so not only did God honor my request, it was paid in full by the company...

Fountain graduated with a 3.5-grade point average with a degree in Organizational Management from the University of Mobile, located in Mobile, Alabama.

"As I walked across the stage, being proud of my accomplishments, God reminded me of my request of allowing my daughter to go to college and for me to attend once she finished. This was a request that I hadn't thought about anymore since that time," Fountain reminisced. "I thank God every day for my daughter because she is the reason I became closer to Him, and I thank Him for remembering my prayer request. God does hear our prayers. We just have to be patient and wait on Him."

" I WAS DENIED ADMISSION, BUT THEN OUT OF NOWHERE, I WAS LATER ACCEPTED BY THE SAME UNIVERSITY

CHRISTINA TUCKER
Fayetteville, Georgia

Ever heard of someone being rejected for admission by a university, only to receive a letter of acceptance eight months later? Well, that's exactly what happened to Christina Tucker, and she says it was only her faith in Christ that made it all possible.

"My faith in God made the impossible, possible," Tucker said. "It was my dream to one day be able to attend a Historically Black University, and Clark Atlanta University was one of the universities that I wanted to attend. I applied for admission in October 2016, but a few weeks later, I received a rejection letter saying that I was not eligible for admission."

But Clark Atlanta University wasn't the only college that denied her admission.

I applied to more than 10 colleges, and I just kept getting rejection letters…

"I was really confused about it all because I made good grades in school, but it seemed like nobody would let me into their school," Tucker recalled, before adding that unlike most of her friends who were also graduating high school and making plans to attend college in the fall of 2017, she on the other hand, while walking across the stage at Fayette County High School Stadium on May 26, 2017 to accept her high school diploma, didn't know if she would attend college in August.

"I felt embarrassed that I hadn't been accepted into college yet, so when everyone kept asking me about my future plans, I acted as if I had plans, but the reality of it was that I didn't have any," Tucker said.

Tucker, however, said that after months of feeling frustrated about not being accepted into school, she decided to stop fighting her circumstances.

"I realized that there was absolutely nothing that I could do about it," Tucker said. "It was out of my control, so I just prayed and put my faith in Jesus Christ to open up a door for me. In fact, on Sunday, June 25, 2017, I got up in front of my church congregation and let everyone know that I didn't know if I would be attending college and that I had turned it all over to God. I felt a release and at peace about it. I just trusted and believed that He would make a way for me, someway, somehow."

The next day, Monday, June 26, 2017, Tucker said a large envelope arrived in the mail with her name on it from Clark Atlanta University.

"I opened it up, and there was a letter that said, "Congratulations, we are pleased to offer you admission into Clark Atlanta University beginning the fall of 2017," Tucker recalled. "I know that it was nobody but God. I didn't do anything extra. I didn't reapply for admission or anything. I just left my rejection as a rejection of admission. This was just amazing. How do you go from being rejected by a school to later being admitted? There's no other way than by placing your faith in God, so for everyone out there wanting to go to college, but your circumstances make it seem impossible, I'm a living testimony that by trusting and placing your faith totally in Christ, it can happen. Just trust Him and watch how He opens a door and makes a way out of no way."

I WAS FACED WITH PAYING $40,000 A YEAR FOR MY CHILDREN TO GO TO COLLEGE & GOD MADE A WAY

According to a recent study conducted by Royall & Company, an organization that conducts over 300 field tests annually across more than 350 partner institutions, more than 40 percent of students who decided not to go the college or university cited the high cost of attendance as the reason why, so it wasn't a surprise to Michael Sam when he found himself trying to find a way to pay $40,000 a year in college tuition.

"I had three children in college all at the same time," Sam said.

His oldest daughter, Justena was enrolled at Baylor University. His son Michael Sam Jr. was enrolled at Rice University, and his youngest daughter, Sharikka, was enrolled at Sam Houston State University.

"My wife and I had all of this on top of our regular bills," Sam recalled. "We always wanted our children to be able to go to the college of their choice. All of my children were admitted into college, but the price of school is very high these days, so between all three of my children, I was faced with paying $40,000 a year in tuition."

All I could do is put my faith in God to make a way...

"I had three children in college on one income, and when I was looking at the numbers on paper, they didn't add up," Sam said, before adding, "I didn't know how I would be able to pay all of it. The only thing I could do is pray and put my faith in God to make a way."

Sam, who has worked at Centerpoint Energy in Houston for more than 30 years, currently serving as Head Journeyman Lineman, supervising over the electrical distribution areas of new construction and restoration, said each time tuition was due while his children were in school during the years of 2009-2013, God always provided a way through unexpected financial resources.

"It seemed like every time tuition was due and I needed extra money in order to pay the tuition, something would come up to where I would get called for more work, resulting in extra pay," Sam said. "Every time it was something unexpected that happened to where what we needed was given to us when we needed it. I can testify that simply looking at the numbers; it's almost unimaginable how you will be able to pay it, but by putting your faith and trust in God, He will make a way out of no way."

All three of Sam's children have graduated from college. Justena graduated with a degree in neuroscience; Michael with a degree in sports management, and Sharikka graduated with a degree in criminal justice and victim studies.

CHAPTER 19
EMPLOYMENT & CAREER

"FOR TRUSTING HIM, GOD TOOK ME FROM ADMINISTRATIVE ASSISTANT TO DIRECTOR

PAMELA NETTER
New Orleans, Louisiana

Like many in corporate America, **Pamela Netter is a hard** worker with a variety of gifts, talents, and the desire to do more, but she says it took a bold step of faith on her part during the summer of 2016 to receive the blessing that God had waiting for her.

Netter was employed as an administrative assistant at a local university, a job in which she says she was grateful for, but being a widow and caring for her 11-year-old son, Joseph, she wanted to move up to a higher-level position with increased pay. Netter, however, said her supervisor didn't feel she had the qualifications and experience to assume a higher role. Disappointed with her supervisor's response, Netter did what she has always done: she went to God for answers.

"I went on a fast," Netter recalled. "I didn't ask God how many days to fast; I just went on a fast until He had given me my answer. I went on the fast on a Monday, and by that Thursday, God had given me my answer."

What she did next is something she had never done before.

I gave my letter of resignation…

"I was nervous, I was a little anxious," Netter explained, before adding, "but the Lord said that He would be my portion and He gave me a scripture: the Lord is a pleasant help in the time of trouble (Psalms 46:1). He was just letting me know that He was going to take care of me no matter what."

Not knowing how she would provide for herself and her son without a job, Netter's last day on her job was June 8, 2016...

"I left my job and just started putting my resume out there," Netter recalled. "Though I didn't have a job, I never missed a car note; I never missed a beat. It was crazy because I was offered every position that I had applied for in between the time I was without a job. It was about a month and a half in which I was without a job, and it was the best month and a half that I've ever had."

Netter was offered a position as a director at First Baptist Academy in Houston, Texas...

"Not only am I a director, but God also gave me an assistant director, and staff, who I am leading, plus He gave me the salary over and above what I asked for," Netter revealed.

She went on to note that to show how good God is, she was also given a position as an adjunct professor at the same employer in which she resigned from, where she was serving as an administrative assistant.

"So from a timespan of June 8, 2016, to August 2016, my life and position totally changed because I put my trust in God and not man," Netter stressed. "I can't even explain it. I know some people were like, you just walked away from a job, but I didn't walk away from a job, I walked into the direction God was leading me. Because of my obedience, not only did He open a door, He opened a window."

Netter said she is a living witness to what God can do when you rely totally on Him, regardless of what it looks like on the outside, even if you don't know what your next move is, and can't see how everything will work out.

"I just watched how God provided for us, even in my anxious moments, He always reminded me to don't worry, trust me,"

Netter said. "I was offered a position as far away as Arizona with the qualifications in which my previous job said they didn't think I had. I've learned that when you put your trust in God and not in man, He will exalt you in due time when you humble yourself under the mighty hand of the Lord."

MY FAITH IN CHRIST TURNED A TEMPORARY POSITION INTO 40 YEARS OF EMPLOYMENT

MARION DENISE FOX
Gautier, Mississippi

I n 1974, wages fell by 2.1 percent and median household income shrunk by $1,500. It was a year of a mild recession, and like many people across the nation, Marion Denise Fox needed a job.

Being a young wife and mother with a child and no college degree, Fox wasn't sure what the future held for her, but she says her faith in Christ proved to be what turned what she thought would be a temporary job, into a long career.

"I was 19 years old looking for a job, so I decided to go down to Ingalls Shipbuilding (in Pascagoula, Mississippi), January 4, 1974," Fox recalled. "They told me they could only guarantee five years of work, and they asked me if I had a problem with that. I told them no, I don't have any problems with that; I just needed a job. My first day on the job was Jan. 7, 1974."

When the fifth year came, all I could do is put my faith in God...
Other people got laid off, but I didn't...

"God blessed me with those five years, plus another 35 years, for a total of 40 years and five months," Fox said.

Just to show how placing your faith and trust in God works, Fox said she was initially hired as a cable assembler.

"I would go on the ship, I was a shipbuilder," she said. "During that same year, I was hired, 1974, we had a strike. I had never been through a strike before, and I didn't know what a strike was. I was new on the job. We were out from December 1974 to sometime in January in 1975, where the union and the company got together to do a contract. Well, when the contract was signed, I was a cable assembler making $2.30 an hour, and I wanted to make more money. I interviewed to get into the B Electrical program, where they had apprentices to be an A or B electrician. I went through the B program, where I could work toward becoming a first-class electrician. I did exactly that. I went on the ship; I learned the trade. I went to school, and I ended up being first class in three years."

Fox noted that during her 40 years at Ingalls Shipbuilding, she was blessed with the opportunity to serve as a supervisor, a union steward, an assistant chief union steward for the union, and also served as an officer for the union for 15 years on the executive board, in addition to nine years as a treasurer of her local union.

"During my time at Ingalls, we built 31 destroyers and battleships," Fox said. "I had a long career, and I just thank God for my career. What started out as temporary employment turned out to be a 40-year career. I give God all the glory for my 40 years, and I encourage anyone out there who may be looking at their individual situation or current employment opportunities to just totally trust God, to put their faith in God, and watch how He'll open up doors. He did that for me. All I could do is trust Him by faith, and He blessed me."

Fox retired from Ingalls Shipbuilding on June 30, 2014.

HAVING FAITH & TRUSTING GOD'S TIMING HAS MADE THE DIFFERENCE IN MY LIFE

SHARRON GOODMAN-HILL
Decatur, Mississippi

Like most college graduates, Sharron Goodman-Hill has always wanted a long, happy and fulfilling career after graduating from college, but once she entered the real world, she says that long-lasting career in which she had always dreamed of didn't start off so well.

"However, because of God's grace I made it through all of the obstacles that I endured, and I am here to proclaim that His mercy, grace, and favor are real," Goodman-Hill said. "After graduating college with a bachelor of science in broadcast journalism from Mississippi Women's University in 1982, I went back to my home town area and worked a myriad of jobs, including substitute teaching, freelance newspaper reporting and also serving as a radio news reporter."

Life was good; however, only after a few months of my radio news reporter job at WOKK/WALT, I was let go; to say that I was devastated is the understatement of the century...

Goodman-Hill said that there was little explanation from management except that they decided to go with a young lady who had worked in that position before she had. At this point in her life, Goodman-Hill said she felt as if she had been handed a lemon and needed to make lemonade, quickly.

"I went on a massive job search after losing the radio job and could find absolutely nothing in my field," Goodman-Hill stressed, before adding, "With the encouragement of my mother, I accepted a shirt factory job. Yes, this college graduate landed a shirt factory job. I was horrible as a shirt folder, and I never made production. One of the most embarrassing moments on that job came one day when my cousin told me very loudly, "Sharron, we used to run right there (pointing to a pole with a speaker) and listen to you when you did your news reports. Embarrassing, humiliating, and humbling are just a few of the emotions I felt while holding back tears that day. However, I kept pressing on and worked dutifully while continuing my journalism job search."

No matter how many interviews I did, nothing came up in my field...

"I heard the Lord say to me during that time (March 1986) that I was not going to have to search hard for a job," Goodman-Hill recalled. "I heard in my spirit that the Lord was going to give me a job. I took another factory job, but I got laid off during the slow season, so I was off searching for a job again."

In the midst of job searching, church involvement, and other things that come with living life, I also became a mother of a beautiful girl, Victoria...

"Being a single mother added an entirely new dimension to an already complicated equation," Goodman-Hill explained. "However, my steps were still being ordered by the Lord. Four years after college, three factory jobs, and a beautiful baby girl later, a breakthrough came my way. The third factory job for this college grad was at Peavey's Electronics in Meridian, Mississippi. Leaving the first day from this highly-coveted job in the local area, with aching hands and tear-filled eyes, I prayed as I was driving home, "Lord, this is my third factory job, what am I supposed to learn from this situation?" I immediately heard in my spirit, "...to humble you." My response was, "Humble me???!!!! I am humble!!!!! I then heard Him ask me, "With that attitude?" I then said, "OK, Lord. Teach me to be humble but hurry up! For the next year, I began to pray more and seek God. I sensed so much peace and joy in my life. I began to be content. This was an amazing time of spiritual growth in my life. I became so content until I started thinking about living in my hometown for the rest of my life. I also began looking into how I could be promoted at Peavey's. I did get a promotion and started working the overnight shift. I was definitely enjoying where I was on the way to where I was going."

Then God provided more options...

"One morning after work, a college friend called me and said she had told a church acquaintance about me and he was going to give me a call about a job at his station," Goodman-Hill recalled. "R.H. Brown of WACR Radio Station in Columbus, Mississippi program, called and made me a job offer that I could not accept. I turned it down flat. I could not live on the amount he offered. After the conversation, I heard in my spirit; you didn't even pray about it. I responded half-heartedly, Ok, Lord. If R. H. Brown calls back, I will pray before I give an answer. I did not think he would call again and felt I had gotten off the hook.

As fate would have it, Brown called back and upped the ante. I wanted to turn him down again, but I kept my vow to God. I told Brown that I needed time to pray before I made my decision. In early October 1988, I began to seek God about this decision; I heard nothing. Finally, Wednesday morning before Thanksgiving in November of 1988, I heard in my spirit, 'Go get your job.' I went to WACR in Columbus, Mississippi, that fall morning with no appointment and unannounced.

Even though I did not have an appointment, Mr. R.H. Brown took me through all of the job formalities. He interviewed me, asked me to do a resume tape, and gave me a station tour. He then informed me that he hired someone because he had not heard from me. I thanked him for his time and headed home."

As Goodman-Hill drove home, she said she felt so much peace, the kind of peace that surpasses all understanding. She felt overjoyed, exceedingly happy, and giddy.

"This is not the norm for someone who just been turned down for a job," Goodman-Hill said. "Instead of feeling down-trodden and depressed, I was experiencing the emotions of one who had just gotten the job. Well, guess what? A few days later, in December 1988, R.H. called me to say that the young lady he hired had just quit. He offered me the job; I accepted and the rest, as they say, is history."

Since that time, Goodman-Hill has been working in broad-cast journalism for more than 30 years. She has had the pleasure of interviewing the likes of Susan Taylor of *Essence Magazine*, best-selling author Pearl Cleage, attorney Walter Bailey, nation-ally and internationally acclaimed actors and actresses, soloists, politicians, former U.S. Attorney Eric Holder, and more.

"The Lord directed my steps on this broadcasting journey after graduating college," Goodman-Hill said. "So when it comes to totally trusting God to rule over my life and placing total faith in Him, I feel that it was the process of my becoming sensitive to the timing and the movement of God that has allowed me to enjoy all of the blessings that I have been able to enjoy."

My message is that regardless of what it looks like, especially for students, who just like me, are looking for careers after college, just trust Him, and the rest will take care of itself…

Goodman-Hill serves as the Director of the Honors Pro-gram and instructor of Mass Communications at Rust College in Holly Springs, Mississippi.

CHAOS WAS EVERYWHERE ON MY JOB, BUT OBEYING GOD'S DIRECTION TO STAY STILL RESULTED IN ONE OF THE BIGGEST BLESSINGS OF MY LIFE

L ike most people, Clifton Franklin has always wanted to have a stable job and a stress-free environment. But a corporate shakeup and layoff on his job at a multi-million dollar oil service company in the early 1980s taught him one of the biggest lessons in his life: that trusting God at His word, regardless of your circumstances, brings an abundance of blessings beyond what you can think or ask.

"My division was the worst performing of all of the divisions that were there," Franklin said. "I was working as an account, and month after month, the company's reports showed how poor our performance was. As a result, a lot of people were being laid off, and we were losing a lot of projects and my question at that time was, Lord, is it time for me to go too? Should I jump ship and leave this company as well?"

That question, Franklin pointed out, is the same question that many people in corporate American ask themselves today when things go south, but he went on to stress that the decision he made concerning his future is a testimony to others on how putting their total trust and faith in God's hands can bring a blessing when a blessing doesn't seem possible with the instructions God gives.

The Lord's directions to me were to stay where I was, and everything would be alright, but it really didn't make sense because month after month people were being laid off, people were leaving...

"I was thinking that it was time for me to go as well," Franklin recalled. "But the thing that kept me there was that several years prior to this, the Lord had given me instructions with a company I was with, and he told me to stay, but I listened to the voice of my friends and just got some bad advice. I left the company, although the Lord was telling me through scripture to stay where I was. That cloud was over my head, and I was determined that when the Lord spoke to me again through His Word, that I was going to obey this time."

The Lord told me that the grass might look greener on the other side, but if you go, you will find out that it's not...

"So I trusted God and stayed there with the company, and sure enough my division did close," Franklin said, before adding, "The way it closed is that all of the people who remained with the company, they found new positions for them. The position they found for me was working in the corporate headquarters in the financial consolidation department. I worked there for probably six months, and then I received a call from the gentleman who used to be the chair of the division at my previous job that ended up folding. He asked if I would be his financial controller. He told me that the reason he chose me is because he watched me during those shaky days at my previous job and he was impressed with my work ethic and the work that I did, and he wanted me to come and join him."

After staying with the company and doing what God told me to do, I started getting promotion after promotion, after promotion...

"This time I trusted God's Word and trusted Him in spite of how I felt, in spite of how things looked, in spite of what people said, and God blessed me," Franklin said. "My career just continued to advance and advance."

Today, Franklin is retired.

FAITH IN CHRIST RESULTED IN ME HAVING A BLESSED CAREER

FANNIE LAMPL

L
ike many people fresh out of high school and on their way to college, Fannie Lampley, in 1965, really didn't know what she wanted to do or be as an adult. The only thing that she knew for sure is that she wanted a little red sports car that she thought she would look good riding in.

However, she says although she didn't have specific plans laid out for her life, her faith in Christ proved to be the only thing she needed to become successful.

"Many people today find themselves wondering or not knowing what it is that they are supposed to do in life," Lampley said, before adding, "But I am a living testimony that when you step out on faith and let God lead you in which direction you should go in life, He will show up."

By trusting God, my life went in a direction that I never ever imagined it would go...

"It was like God kept sending people my way to help point me in the direction that I should go," Lampley said, before adding that after completing her bachelor's degree from Rust College in Holly Springs, Mississippi, she had a chance encounter with a respected educator from the University of Mississippi who saw that she had a gift for speaking and encouraged her to further her education. Although she didn't know what opportunities would present itself after continuing her education, she said she simply put her faith in God to open a door when the time came for her to need a door to be opened.

"I prayed to God, and He heard my prayer," she said.

In 1990 I became the first women as dean of students at Rust College...

"This was an amazing thing to happen to me, and I know it was only the favor of God that made it all possible," Lampley stressed. "There is no way that I could have accomplished any of this without trusting God with my life and my career."

Lampley worked for Rust College for 30 years and is now the director of public relation at ICS Headstart in Holly Springs, Mississippi.

COACHING WAS A GOD-SENT ASSIGNMENT FOR ME

HENRY T. HOOD
Holly Springs, Mississippi

F or more than three decades, Henry Hood has given out game day assignments to more than 700 basketball players he has coached, but he says the assignment that God gave him in 1989 has made all the difference in his life.

"It was definitely a faith walk for me," said Hood. "As far as coaching, I never had a desire to even go into education, period. I never wanted to be in education. I was actually going to go into law enforcement."

Hood, a slender, 6-foot-3 inch tall man, said God rerouted what he wanted, which was a career in law enforcement and opened a door as a coach at CADET Junior High School in Holly Springs, Mississippi, on August 18, 1981, a day in which he says he'll never forget.

"When the job became available at CADET, I went for an interview; they hired me, and that probably was the best thing that could have ever happened to me," said Hood. "I've been in coaching for 39 years between two schools, CADET and Byhalia Middle School in Byhalia, Mississippi. I've enjoyed every minute of it. You could say that coaching was a God-sent assignment of faith for me."

Not knowing what God had in store for him, Hood said he made the decision to trust the way in which God was leading him in his career.

"We often have plans or ideas on what we want to do with our lives, but it really all comes down to what it is that God wants us to do with our lives and what He has designed for our lives. At the time, I couldn't see all of the blessings that God had waiting for me as a coach."

As a coach, Hood won four boys division conference championships; five pee wee (4th-6th grade) boys championships; three girls conference championships and five runner-up conference championships. Hood also was fortunate to coach CADET's track team, where dozens won medals on the local, state, and even the national level at Hershey's Track & Field Games, a competition created in 1975, the largest youth sports program of its kind in the United States and Canada.

"People always ask me why I didn't want to go to the next level (college, or pro) to coach," Hood said while reflecting on his coaching career. "For me, it really wasn't about that, moving up. It was about the lives that I was able to touch during my years of coaching. So many of the boys and girls who I've coached have gone on to become productive citizens and many of the lessons taught through the game of basketball and track, carry over into the real world. I retired in May 2018, so looking back at everything, it was a total faith walk to trust that God knew what was best for my life, and He did. My life has been enriched and fulfilled, but I can say that it was all because I trusted Him."

Hood, who graduated with a Bachelor of Science degree in Health, Physical Education, Recreation and Dance from Mississippi Industrial College in Holly Springs, Mississippi in 1978, noted that his testimony is for those who are not sure about which direction to go in their career to completely trust God by placing their lives in God's hands.

"Sometimes there are blessings you can't see coming, but God does," Hood said.

BY TRUSTING & LISTENING TO GOD, I WAS BLESSED WITH A NEW JOB

ASHLEY

Lithon

Regardless of who you are, where you come from, or what you do for a living, there's one thing that no one is immune to: problems.

And when a multitude of problems all of a sudden came into the life of Ashley Payne, she admits that she wanted to give up. She wanted to wallow in her sorrow, and she questioned whether there was still hope for her life. However, it was during this time in which she learned that trusting God and being obedient to what He wanted is how she received her biggest breakthrough.

"2016 was a tremendously trying year," Payne recalled. "It started in January when it was discovered while at the doctor's office that some tumors that I had removed in 2009 had reoccurred. As a result of this, I had to decide whether having surgery would affect me being able to have a child later in life. In the midst of me trying to decide what to do, whether to get rid of the tumors and any other viable options, I lost my job as an attorney. Losing my job meant losing my health insurance. The same week that I lost my job—I had been dating someone for four and a half years—that person and I split, so during the week of February 14, 2016, a lot came crashing down on my head."

My life felt like it could not get any worse...

"I was living with my mother at the time, and she was the sole provider for our household, and in the month of March 2016 while I was still trying to find new employment, my mom became incredibly ill and was hospitalized and had to have emergency surgery," Payne recalled. "The way her job is set up, she only gets a very few paid days off. So in our house, we're wondering what's going to happen if the sole breadwinner can't work. I'm unemployed, not to mention the stress of having a parent who needs emergency surgery, and the doctors can't figure out what's wrong."

It really, really felt like all the things that could go wrong, did...

"In addition to that, all of the cars in our house, my car, my little brother's car, my mom's car, everybody's car broke down at some point in 2016," Payne said, before adding that problems came so often that it seemed comical.

"I was told things like, oh, you need a completely new engine, and the funny part was that I already knew that the kind of car I had sometimes have problems, so I had an extended warranty, but when I needed a new engine, something that the extended warranty would cover, I was told that my warranty had just expired last month," Payne said. "Of course, I would talk to my mentors about how I felt. I was so close to my breaking point because everything was just happening and I felt like I had worked so hard in my life to be the person to put myself in a position so that I could navigate my way through challenges. My mentor would just look at me and laugh because he knew that's how God works, and that is the building blocks of our faith when things like that happen."

Payne noted that it's easier for us to praise God and to be thankful, to be happy, to be joyous, to be reliant, and to talk about God's goodness when things are going well in our lives. However, she stressed that it becomes increasingly more complex, especially for someone like herself who is a planner, a person who likes to know what's happening all of the time and to be in control of things.

"I had to learn how to rely on God when things started to seemingly fall apart," Payne said.

It pushed me in such a way and moved me toward God in a way that I had never in my entire life experienced...

"I had gotten so low that I felt like I must have done something wrong and that I didn't deserve to be the recipient of grace anymore, and if God felt that way, I wasn't going to make any more requests to change my circumstances, or for Him to fix what was going on in my life," Payne said. "I was going to wallow in all of the nastiness and all of the hurt, all of the pain, all of the disappointment, all of the discouragement. I was just going to stay there. I wasn't going to pray about it anymore, so that's where I was toward the middle part of the year of 2016. I was like; this is God's desire for me. God's desire for me is to suffer, so I'm just going to suffer. I'm just going to be unhappy, and I'm going to be sad, and I'm going to cry all the time because obviously, this is what I deserve."

I'm very active on Facebook... and guess what God instructed me to do? To go on Facebook and publicly share all of these problems I was experiencing...

She says God commanded her to share and tell everyone about her lowest moments, to tell people about all of the days she wanted to give up, and even the days in which she felt so low that she was unable to get out of bed.

"God wanted me to share all of that," said Payne. "So I said, sure God, I'll share it...as soon as I have a job. Once I have a job, I'm going to share that. And God said that's not what I said. I want you to share it now. And I'm like, NO, because that doesn't make for a good story, not to mention my ego. I can't get on Facebook and say, look at all of the bad stuff that happened to me, and how hurtful everything was and not be able to tie it up with a nice bow saying I lived happily ever after, that I got a job, and I moved out of my mom's home, and all of these things. I can't share it until it's perfect like that at the end."

Payne said the New Year came, January 2017, and even though she had made it up in her mind to have a more positive outlook and not feel down on herself or defeated, she still hadn't taken the next step of sharing her story on Facebook like God had commanded her to do.

"I still hadn't gotten a job, I wasn't even getting job interviews, and finally God was like, I am sick of you, here's what I've asked you to do and you still haven't done it," Payne recalled.

So one day in March 2017, I finally decided to be obedient, and through faith, I wrote out the longest, most personal Facebook post that I had ever written...

"So many people contacted me publicly, privately, via text message, and phone calls to share their story with me, telling me how they had been dealing with the same thing and how sharing my story with them on Facebook made them feel encouraged or made a difference and let them know that they weren't alone," Payne said.

The next week, God blessed me with a job. The very next week! I hadn't even had any job interviews. Not one! I couldn't even get a callback...

"So my lesson was in faith and obedience," Payne said. "You have to trust Him, even when it looks really bad, when it looks like everything is crashing down, we should endure. God never leaves us. God never forsakes us. God loves us. God will even appoint people to come speak to us if we need it. It's not whether or not God gave us the power to end suffering in the world. It's whether we're bold enough to use it. God absolutely equipped us with the power to change the world. It's just that we haven't tapped into it yet, or we refuse to do so, or that we're disobedient. Just trust Him and do what He says. I did and look at what He did for me. What He did for me, He can do for you too."

Payne, a 2013 graduate of Emory University School of Law, was hired as an attorney to serve in the Community Prosecution Office of the Fulton County District Attorney's Office in Atlanta.

I LOST MY JOB AFTER
19 YEARS OF EMPLOYMENT

RICKY ALLEN JOHNSON
Moss Point, Mississippi

As the Sunday School Superintendent at Union Baptist Church in Pascagoula, Mississippi, Rickey Johnson has spent years teaching churchgoers to trust God regardless of their circumstances, but when he lost his job in 2009, with a wife and two children depending on him to provide for them, he says it was his faith in Christ that allowed him to make it through.

"I'm a structural welder by trade," Johnson said of his job at Ingalls Shipbuilding, located in Pascagoula, Mississippi. "I was welding all morning, and when I got through with a certain task, I sat down on my lunch box, and I dozed off on my job. I fell asleep."

While I was asleep, two supervisors walked in and all of a sudden Johnson found himself in a place in which he had never been in.

They fired me...

"I had a meeting with the supervisors, and they asked me if there was anything I wanted to say," Johnson recalled. "I said no. I couldn't say anything. I couldn't tell them I had a daughter in college, a child in private school, a house note, car note, light bill. I couldn't say anything."

However, Johnson, now unemployed, said as he walked from the job in which he had held since 1990, something happened as he headed to his vehicle in which he will never forget. Someone whom he had never met in his life gave him a word of encouragement.

"He asked me where I was going," Johnson explained. "I told him that they let me go. He said God must have something better for you. Because of that, I was able to walk out of the yard and not get depressed. At this point, I decided to just place my faith in God, because God is the one who gave me the job in 1990, and I just told myself that if God wanted to wake me up, He would have woke me up that day."

Sometimes God has to fire you from one place to get you to somewhere else...

Johnson said he began to lean on God and trust that he and his family would make it.

"And we did, in fact, I actually gained weight after I was fired from my job," said Johnson, who has always been slender in stature. But during this time, the Lord showed me something. He said I fired you for a reason. I've been asking you to teach the Fatherhood class. God had been asking me for years to teach it. Well, I started teaching it while I was out of work."

The class, called Fatherhood 24/7, is offered through the Jackson County Mississippi Civic Action. The purpose is to strengthen families of all backgrounds and life circumstances by providing parenting education and support through seminars, workshops, and consultations.

"I started going to the high schools and prisons teaching the fatherhood class," Johnson explained. "I started teaching the class and started liking it."

Then, all of a sudden, Ingalls, the job I got fired from called...

"They called to offer me my job back," Johnson said. They asked if I could come on Thursday. I said no, I have a graduating class, my Fatherhood class. The person on the phone said what? I said I have a graduating class on Thursday and I politely got off the phone. My wife asked me who was that? Told her that it was the union man calling to give me my job back, but I told him I could not come on Thursday. My wife said, what? I told her, you know I can't go because I have a graduating class on Thursday. Well, the union man called again while I was talking to my wife, and asked if I could be there on Friday. I said, yes, I could be there Friday. I came in that Friday, and they gave me my job back."

Johnson, who was out of work for 10 months, said his faith in God had allowed his circumstances to come full circle, while he did what God wanted him to do.

"A man in my first class that graduated put it in perspective for me. I told him that I used to be a structural welder," Johnson recalled. "The man told me you're still a welder. Now you're welding men's lives back together. You see, the Lord blessed me with the opportunity to teach this class, and He has even blessed me on my job. Today, I'm the apprentice coordinator for Ingalls. God restored me. Everything that I lost, God gave it back to me, and more. My lights have never been off. I've never been hungry. Both my girls have graduated from college. I'm blessed. My testimony is for anyone who finds themselves out of a job, regardless of the reason why, just place your faith and trust in Him, and you'll see that He has something better in store for you. Today, I'm better."

I WAS A TEEN MOM, BUT THROUGH FAITH, I'VE ACCOMPLISHED A LOT

ERICA STEWART
Prichard, Alabama

E rica Stewart became a mother at the age of 17, something in which she says some people believed nothing good would ever come of her life due to her circumstances, but by placing her faith in God, she says her life has been so blessed that she has even made history on her job.

"I never went to college, but God has blessed my life," Stewart said.

The job of a mother, according to Stewart, is being able to provide for her child, and she says by trusting God, she has been able to do just that, while having a successful career in a male-dominated industry at Ingalls Shipbuilding in Pascagoula, Mississippi.

"I never wanted to work at the shipyard," Stewart stressed, before adding, "It was not my dream. However, God had a purpose for me. I went there to Ingalls Shipbuilding's Employment Office in 1997 with a friend who asked if I wanted to ride over with her to fill out an application. I said I will ride with you, but I'm not interested in a job. I went along for the ride. My friend brought out a thick stack of application papers. At the time, there were no computer applications. My friend gave me a pen and I kind of played around with it in the car, taking my time filling out the application. I half did the application, and gave it to her, my friend. I had no experience; I knew nothing about the shipyard. I gave my application to her out of the window of the car. She took it in but came back saying they wanted to interview me now. Sitting there in sweat pants, I got out of the car, I walk into the employment office, and to my surprise, I did an amazing interview."

They hired me on the spot...

"That's the good news, the bad news is that they didn't hire my friend," Stewart revealed. "I went home telling my mom that I got a job at the shipyard, still not knowing what it was. I started the job there at Ingalls."

Working in a male-dominated industry, Stewart says she felt that the enemy did not want her there at Ingalls Shipbuilding due to various trials she encountered. She survived several rounds of massive layoffs and even sustained an eye injury where metal was logged into her eye, giving her many reasons to quit. However, she says she decided to continue to listen to the voice of God to stay there.

"I went through a very, very tough time there, but God had me there for a reason," Stewart proclaimed. "God had an assignment for me. I would go home many nights praying for the Lord to give me the strength to make it. I just kept fighting."

As scared as I was, I just trusted Him to make a way...

While in the hospital receiving treatment for the eye injury she sustained, Stewart said she was given a new job assignment just at the right time, switching from being a ship fitter to welding.

"When I came back to work from my eye injury, my boss at the time had planned to terminate me," Stewart recalled. "He said, 'I don't think this is going to work out for you. As a matter of fact, I'll go ahead and give you a pink slip. Maybe you should try something else, work behind a desk or something, maybe Walmart.' I told him, I do agree with you. Ship fitting is not for me; however, I will still be working here at the shipyard, because thanks to God, I will be moving into welding on Monday. I tell you, he had a look on his face like there was no tomorrow, because he had been defeated. What he set out to do of getting rid of me, he couldn't, because God was in control the entire time. You see, what the enemy meant for my bad, God turned it around for my good."

Since being hired at Ingalls Shipbuilding in 1997, Stewart has been afforded a variety of opportunities in which she says is only because of her faith in God, and her trust in His guidance for her life and career.

"As for my career, I have been involved with the union, I now do recruiting, I was the union steward, assistant chief steward, chief steward, elected in as the president, and I've now been appointed as the very first black woman International Representative for the International Brotherhood of Boilermakers," said Stewart. "My testimony is that God saw something in me, and God showed favor in me to allow me an opportunity to be there. As a teen mom, I'm a living witness that through faith in Him, God can do the same in anyone else's life. Just trust Him."

I MOVED TO ANOTHER STATE WITH NO JOB IN ORDER TO PURSUE MY DREAM CAREER

ERIC ELLIOT
Richmond, Texas

E ric Elliot has always wanted to work in medical and pharmaceutical sales; however, back in 2004, there was virtually
no opportunity for this kind of career in Jackson, Mississippi,
where he lived. But he says he made a decision to step out on
faith and move to Houston, Texas in hopes of finding employment in medical and pharmaceutical sales.

"There was no guarantee that I would get a job by going to
Houston," Elliot said. "The Bible says faith is the substance of
things hoped for, the evidence of things not seen. I couldn't see
what would happen by leaving Jackson and going to Houston,
but I went. I was someone coming out of college, Jackson State
University, with zero experience in the industry."

Elliot, with a small amount of money he had saved up,
moved to Houston, with the understanding that he would have
to find employment quickly.

"I started working within a month after I moved to Houston," Elliot said. "I was hired by Enterprise Rent-A-Car. It was
crazy because my first day at Enterprise, I met a guy named
Nate. We were basically in suits washing cars. He was like, man
if I were you, I would start looking for a new job because this is
not what you want to do. Nate and I became friends after we discovered that we had some common interests. Both of us wanted
to break into the medical industry in sales."

While Elliot was working at Enterprise Rent-A-Car, he
says it was only the hand of God that could have ordered his
steps.

"I began to come in contact with many representatives
working within the pharmaceutical industry as a result of the

company's car policy," Elliot explained. "I quickly discovered that there were certain fleet companies that would handle car rentals for pharmaceutical reps, so I would take it upon myself to handle their reservations personally, but at the same time, it gave me an opportunity to interview them on what they did to get into the industry to secure a job. There were quite a few people that were placed in my path; some of those people were able to get me interviews with some really big companies."

But while Elliot's eyes were on breaking into the medical and pharmaceutical sales industry, he excelled at Enterprise Rent-A-Car.

"I continued to climb the ladder at Enterprise and continued to get promoted," Elliot said. "After one year at Enterprise, my fiancé and I got married in 2005. I continued working at Enterprise, but internally, I was thinking to myself that it's taking forever to break into this pharmaceutical sales game. But what ended up happening is that I received another promotion at Enterprise, an opportunity to manage one of the largest branches. Well, shortly after I got that position, I had another job offer for what I've always wanted to do: break into medical sales."

I had to make a decision...

Elliot, in 2007, was faced with deciding whether to continue his career at Enterprise Rent-A-Car, where he was excelling, or follow his dream, which he didn't know for sure how it would turn out. Now with a wife, in which he promised to provide for, this was a big decision to make. He decided to follow his dream and started working for Medline Industries, the largest privately-held manufacturer and distributor of medical and surgical supplies in the United States.

"Here I am having this goal in mind to move to Houston to break into pharmaceutical sales, and I end up doing one better by getting into medical device sales," Elliot said, before adding, "Since that time, it has been nothing but a blessing because not only have I been able to get into a position to where I'm able to help people while knowing that these products I'm selling can save lives, when I wake up every day, I'm excited to go into work, because it's always something different."

Elliot noted that he feels especially blessed because he not only stepped out on faith to follow his dream, he also recognizes that he is one of the few chosen to work in the medical and pharmaceutical sales.

"You don't see a lot of black people in the industry, so what this has given me is an opportunity," Elliot said. "Every time I feel like it's becoming tough, or I feel like I had some issues to deal with, or if I don't know how I'm going to get through it, I've always been able to bring those problems to the altar. I'm so blessed."

Since I moved here to Texas, I have never experienced a layoff, never fired from a position, and that in itself is something because in the industry I'm in, it becomes vulnerable...

"In this industry, often time companies get acquired, product lines get dissolved, or they may sell off parts of the company," Elliot stressed. "However, I've been able to be a provider for my family. I've been able to do a lot of great things, see some of the world, share it with my family, help others, and save lives in the process. It was all made possible by faith."

Today, Elliot is a pharmacy specialist at Baxter Healthcare Corporation in Houston.

CHAPTER 20
VEHICLE ACCIDENTS

GOD SAVED MY LIFE

ZACHARY LAVALLIES
Houston, Texas

Zachary LaVallies has always dreamed of living a long life, but a car accident in 1989, made him realize that the reason he is still here is no accident.

"In 1989 I was living life on my own terms," LaVallies said. "I had just started to get into church, but I wasn't saved. I was going through the motions mainly because at the time my girlfriend's uncle was the pastor of the church. Every time they would open the doors of the church, I could feel her uncle looking at me as though he was saying, what are you waiting for? Every Sunday, I would not accept the invitation to Christ. This went on for quite some time. I just didn't have the desire to take that walk. I loved living in the fast lane."

But in a split second, LaVallies said, his life was changed.

"One day in November of 1989, I was on the way to Greens Point Mall (located in Houston) to pay on my suit I had in lay-a-way before I went to work," said LaVallies, a man whose wardrobe has always been important to him.

While driving through the parking lot, I blacked out behind the wheel of my car...

"My friend was in the car with me, and by his account, my hands gripped the wheel and would not let go," LaVallies said. "We began to speed through the parking lot near Montgomery Wards (a retail store), and my friend made a choice. Since my foot was glued to the gas pedal and my hands gripped the wheel, and the automotive center was straight ahead and full of customers, my friend turned the wheel just enough that we slammed into a parked car. When I finally came to my senses, I was sitting in the back of an ambulance being checked out."

LaVallies said the 1979 Cougar he was driving was totaled.

"That car was so smashed up that when my mother and girlfriend arrived on the scene, they assumed the worst," LaVallies recalled.

They thought that there was no way I could have survived and if I did, I would probably be in bad shape, but when they walked to the back of the ambulance they saw me sitting up in one piece with no broken bones, no cuts or bruises, neither was my friend hurt...

LaVallies said the car accident is proof that there is a God and that God loves each of us. He says his faith was strengthened as a result of the accident, an accident that could have ended his life.

"That following Sunday when they opened the doors of the church, it was like something just lifted me up out my seat and the next thing I knew I was shaking the pastor's hand and saying I accept Jesus as my savior," LaVallies said, before adding, "I believe in Jesus' death, burial and resurrection and I wanted to be baptized. I realize now that God had a plan for my life: God called me to the ministry. I went from running from God to preaching God's Word. That was the day God saved my life."

WITH GOD, I SURVIVED A MAJOR CAR ACCIDENT

BEVERLY WILLIAMS
Pascagoula, Mississippi

I t was the summer of 2001, one year after she and her husband Vincent, divorced. It was one of the most difficult times in Beverly Williams' life, where various trials seemed to appear and reappear in her life, but she says it was a horrific accident that left her in rehab for more than nine months, with no job, no money, and nowhere else to turn except her faith Jesus Christ for help.

"I was driving, and out of nowhere, I was hit by a truck," Williams recalled. "I was rushed to the hospital, and when I got to the hospital, I blacked out during surgery. When I woke up, I had tubes in my mouth and everywhere else. I couldn't walk, I couldn't do anything except lay there. I was in the hospital for 11 days, but when I left, I still couldn't walk."

Although I couldn't physically walk, I decided to walk by faith...

"I just started reading and studying my Bible and taking God at His Word and applying His Word to my life," Williams said. I didn't have money, so I asked for it, and He gave it to me. During this time, I wasn't working, and my daughter was going to college, and she needed a car. I prayed to God, and He made a way for that to happen. God supplied all of my needs through people."

Williams stressed that she is a living witness that just as it is with stories in the Bible, her faith in God made her well.

"I not only survived this accident, but my body was also healed, and all of my needs were met," Williams said. "Although I didn't personally have the means for all of my needs to be met; that was God meeting my needs, and for that, to God be the glory."

Williams went on to note that what wowed her the most during this time, is that she and her husband reunited.

"We remarried in 2012," Williams said. "I went through so many trials and tribulations, but the one thing that I know is that it was only by putting my faith in God that I am where I am today with a healed body, a closer relationship with God, and my husband and three children are a family again."

TRUSTING GOD

EARNESTINE S
Holly Springs, Mi

J oshua 1:9 says, "Be strong and courageous. Do not be afraid; do not be discouraged; for the Lord, your God will be with you wherever you go."

Growing up, I often heard adults make two statements about God, "He may not come when you want him, but he's right on time," and, "God spoke to me." To the former, I'd think if he doesn't come when you want him he is not on time because on time is when you want help, and to the later, I would smile thinking—you told yourself what you wanted to hear. One cold and dark night on a lonely road, I changed my way of thinking about those two statements.

One rainy Sunday afternoon, I tried with no avail to find someone to drive my husband to the airport for an out-of-town meeting. With the clock ticking, I realized that I would have to do it myself. I never was comfortable driving in the dark or in the rain. Just as I put the two, four, and six-year-old in the car, my husband announced he would drive there, and I could drive back.

As we neared the airport, I decided that I would drop him off at the door and make a fast getaway home before dark. It didn't happen. The children asked if they could go inside to see Daddy's plane, and Daddy said yes.

When we returned to the car, the children asked if we could go to McDonald's. Begging made me acquiesce so, I turned left instead of right when I came to the highway. By the time we left McDonald's, it was dark. The baby had been acting sickly all day and had started to cry again.

I broke my own rule of safety and took him out of his car seat and brought him up front with me. I got back on the highway and fed him French fries. When my darling baby finished the last French fry, he crawled over to me, pulled himself up, put his arm around my neck and caught hold of the steering wheel, and made an attempt to sit on my lap.

A car came up behind me with lights on bright, interfering with my vision. I slowed my speed and managed to get my baby out my lap and back on the seat with his head and hands away from me. "Please go around me," I said out loud. Instead, the car hit me from behind and sent me speeding toward a wet mud covered part of the road where trucks had been coming in and out of an unpaved road. I came to this small bridge and discovered that I was losing control of the car. I went from one side to the other igniting sparks on the way.

I looked ahead in horror and counted five sets of car lights. "Help me please, Lord. I don't know what to do." Before I could take a breath a clear and present voice said, "You'll be all right; get your baby."

Without hesitation, I told the children on the back to get down on the flood and stay down. With my left hand, I steered the car, with the other I brought my baby to my chest, and at that very moment, this calm voice said, "Hit your breaks." I had been taught not to do that, but I did exactly that.

My car spent around three times and headed back toward the airport left the road, went down a hill and hit the only tree on the bank of a creek filled with running water.

"Mommy, Mommy, get off me." I came to realize that I had gone across the seat, with my baby in tow and landed on my daughter that was huddled on the floor. I rolled onto the glass filled seat and opened the back door and helped my daughter out the car. Kissing my oldest son, I said to him, "Sweetheart, we came through trees. I can't carry all three of you at the same time. Can you be brave while Mommy take your sister and brother up the hill?" without crying, he said, "Yes, I'll wait right here for you to come back, Mommy."

With my baby in one arm and my daughter in the other, I reached the highway. "Stay here; I'll be right back," I said as I placed the baby in my daughter's care. At that moment a car stopped and asked if anyone was hurt and announced that he would go call the police. I headed back for my son.

"I wasn't scared Mommy." my bright-eyed child told me, "I knew you would be back." As I retraced my steps back up the hill, I could feel two thankful hearts beating a simultaneous rhythm.

When my husband returned home, he took me to see the car that had been classified as total. The door where my baby head would have been had we stayed on the front seat had been pushed in touching that very place. The seat itself had moved forward and upbringing the space of itself within inches of the steering wheel. I stood there how right the old people in my community were. From that night forward I have believed that God does what God said he would do in Isiah 65:24, "Before they call I will answer; while they are still speaking I will hear."

CHAPTER 21

SUPPLYING DAILY NEEDS

"

GOD MADE A WAY FOR US TO TAKE CARE OF 45 PEOPLE IN OUR HOME FOR 60 DAYS AFTER HURRICANE KATRINA

KEVIN REED
Houston, Texas

T he day before Katrina hit, New Orleans Mayor Ray Nagin on Sunday, August 28, 2005, issued the city's first-ever mandatory evacuation order, but little did Kevin Reed, who is originally from New Orleans and living in Houston at the time know that his faith in God was about to be tested like it had never been before.

"We had over 45 people living in our house for more than 60 days," said Reed. "There was a mass exodus from New Orleans, and everyone was trying to get to higher ground. Having your mom to stay in your house is one thing, but when you add aunts, uncles, brothers, sisters and their kids, that's a different thing. There were no more hotels available in the surrounding area and throughout Houston, so my wife and I had to take in over 45 people into our home. It was a mix of my family and my wife's side of the family. We had my mother, I had my sisters and brothers, their husbands and wives, and children and then my wife's parents, her grandparents, uncles, and aunts and a host of cousins. Our lives changed tremendously just on that Sunday afternoon."

Hurricane Katrina struck New Orleans early in the morning on Monday, August 29. Hundreds of thousands of people in Louisiana, Mississippi, and Alabama were displaced from their homes, and experts estimate that Katrina caused more than $100 billion in damage.

"We have always been giving people, so of course we couldn't turn people away," said Reed, whose home is approximately 2,700 square feet in size. "There wasn't any other place for them to go."

We had people everywhere; we even had people sleeping in our bedroom...

"Whatever space was vacant, it had a person in it, we got everyone situated, and Katrina hit," Reed recalled. "It looked like everything was going to be ok, but then the levees broke, and life changed for them, and life changed for us because now we had 45 people in our home that didn't have a place to go."

My wife and I had taken it upon ourselves to provide them with food and shelter. Of course, that taxed our resources to the max; We went from trying our best to provide food for ourselves and two children to trying to figure out how we were going to feed 45 additional people...

"We had to provide food for them, and we didn't ask them for anything simply because they would have to use what they had for when they returned home in New Orleans," Reed said. "To ask them to foot the bill for anything would have been self-ish. We had to make meals that would stretch—spaghetti, beans, things like that."

It took a lot of soul-searching, a lot of praying; sometimes, I thought I was going to lose my mind; It was a struggle just to get up and go to work...

"I had to tell my supervisors that I'm here, but I'm not here," said Reed. "I was worried about the senior citizens that were with us. We had to make sure that everyone had their medications and that everybody was mentally healthy. I said all of that to say that God has not put us here just for ourselves, and sometimes He reveals that to us in situations such as this. Had I not had the upbringing in Christ that I had, I probably would have told them, no you can't come here, go up the road, because I can't be bothered with you all, but I could not do that. My spirit wouldn't allow me to do that."

My faith in God opened the door for Him to provide...

Reed said as money became tight, he and his wife prayed to God for help keeping their individual household together with bills and necessities, and additional resources to help them feed the 45 people living in their home for months.

"Our local church, our places of employment, and other places donated gift cards and things to help us purchase groceries and the things we needed," Reed said. "That was God working through people to bless us and to bless those under our care after Katrina hit. We didn't know how we were going to get through this, but by having faith and trust in God, we made it. Everybody transitioned someplace, and God gets the glory because we didn't lose anybody. Nobody was killed in the storm; the only thing that was lost was earthy possessions, some material things. Had I not been as grounded as I was in my faith, and knowing who God is, and understanding what He has for us to do as Christians, I would not have made it. I think that if Christians knew our purpose and why we are here, then this world would be a better place. I've learned the lesson that we are not here for ourselves. Sometimes you don't learn until you get pushed into the fire, and that was my trial by fire. I have learned so much from that experience. My wife and I gained so much more, not only as a couple, but as Christians from that experience, and how we were able to let our faith grow through that entire process. It wasn't easy by no means, and I wouldn't wish it on my worst enemy. I think if God had chosen us to do it again, we would."

I TRUSTED & GOD PROVIDED

VERONICA JARMON
Fayetteville, Georgia

I t was the summer of 1984. **Veronica Jarmon had recently** given birth to her second child, Michael. Because she was not working, Veronica fixed home-cooked meals for the family and prepared fresh homemade baby food for Michael when he began the transition to eating regular food.

The young family traveled when they desired and received help from parents and other family members when needed. However, at one point, Veronica wanted to do more to help her family financially. She considered getting a job, but she ultimately felt that God was leading her to stay at home to care for the family's two young children.

I decided to simply go on faith and trust that God would bless us, and He did, in an unlikely way…

Jarmon said that during that summer of 1984, her husband's uncle and aunt from Summerville, South Carolina came to Atlanta to visit the family. Her husband's aunt, according to Jarmon, had a cousin who lived in the Atlanta area, so Jarmon and her husband invited the cousin to come over to visit, as well. While visiting, the cousin whom Jarmon had never met before, noticed that she and her husband had a young child and asked what kind of formula they used to feed their son, Michael.

"I said ProSobee (Enfamil)," Jarmon recalled.

It turned out that the cousin was a distributor of ProSobee baby formula. He informed Jarmon and her husband of his intention to supply the family with the formula, saying, "I can get you as much formula as you need, for as long as you need it. All you have to do is come to my house and get it."

We never had to buy ProSobee from that moment on…

"I believe that was God's provision for our son," Jarmon said, before adding, "We didn't have to spend any more money on formula. That was truly amazing. He (the cousin) could have assumed that I breastfed my son, but God allowed him to open his mouth and not only ask, but also freely give us the formula we fed our son. My story of faith is that when you put your faith in God, He will provide."

Michael, an Army veteran, and former commercial airline pilot serves today as a college aviation instructor in the Pacific Northwest.

GOD PROVIDED RUNNING WATER FOR MY FAMILY

EVERLYNN GOFF
Crenshaw, Mississippi

For Everlynn Goff, it's the little things that God has done in her life that have left her knowing without a shadow of a doubt that there is a reward for putting your faith in God, just as Hebrews 11:6 promises.

One of those little things that God has done for Goff happened when she was 15 years old during a severe whether freeze in 1974 in her hometown of Crenshaw, Mississippi. The temperature, according to Goff, was below zero degrees, something that doesn't often happen in Crenshaw, Mississippi. During these rare occasions, the protocol is to leave the water faucet running overnight to ensure that there would be running water the next day.

"But this particular time I mistakenly turned the water off, so the next day on Saturday morning, we got up, and all of the water was frozen," Goff explained.

Goff recalls her step-father outside trying to unthaw the water trying a variety of methods known to help unthaw frozen water and frozen water pipes, but nothing worked.

I remember going to the window in the front of the house, and I began to pray...

"I asked the Lord to please let the water come back on so that my family would have water," Goff recalled, before adding, "Within 10 minutes and with the outside temperature still below freezing, water began to flow out. God provided water for my family."

Goff said she knows that God heard her prayer and that it was her faith that put things in motion for God to restore the water for her family during their time of need.

"This is just one testimony of so many times where I've seen God move because of my faith, my prayer, and my belief in Him," Goff said.

GOD PROVIDED A ROOF OVER MY HEAD

RENEE THOMPSON

The year 2013 is a year that Renee Thompson will never forget. That year, her home was flooded, losing 80 percent of her possessions due to water damage, leaving her with no home and no place to go.

"I came home that day, and the entire house was flooded with water," Thompson said. "I never expected to walk in and see what I saw. I was renting the home, and due to the water damage, I couldn't stay there."

I had nowhere to go, and I didn't know how things would work out for me...

"I didn't have a place to stay, and I didn't know where to go, so all I could do is put my faith in God to help me," said Thompson, who at one point was actually living in her car. "It seemed like help wasn't coming fast enough, so I began to pray to God, and I believed that He would help me."

Thompson said as a result of her faith; God opened a door for her through a family friend.

"I was introduced to a house through my brother's girlfriend, and by the grace of God, I was able to get the house," Thompson said. "As Christians, we know that God watches over us, but sometimes we go through things that really do test our faith in Him. It was during this circumstance that I placed all of my faith and trust in Christ, and I know that God is real. I knew that it was only God who opened this door for me. It was so overwhelming. I had no place to go, but God provided a roof over my head. My testimony of faith is that for anyone who finds themselves in a place where they don't see a way out or a place where they don't know what to do, just trust Him to take care of you, to provide for you, and He will. Look at what He did for me."

CHAPTER 22
MIRACLES

GOD HEALED MY ARTERIES

JOHNNY DA

Holly Springs, M

Undergoing major surgeries and medical procedures is something that Johnny Daniels has always heard friends and family talk about, but when he was told that he needed major surgery on his arteries in 2012, he says it was his faith in Christ that healed him.

"The doctor told me I had to have a stent put in my heart," Daniels recalled. "I got worried, and I didn't know what I was going to do. I didn't want a stent, but it was totally out of my control. All I could do is pray and ask God to heal me from not having the stent put in me."

A stent is a small mesh tube that's used to treat narrow or weak arteries that carry blood away from your heart to other parts of your body.

A stent, according to the National Heart, Lung, and Blood Institute, is placed in an artery as part of a procedure called percutaneous coronary intervention (PCI), also known as coronary angioplasty. PCI restores blood flow through narrow or blocked arteries.

I prayed to God the night before my scheduled surgery, I prayed to God in the morning of the surgery, and prayed to God when I was at the hospital...

Daniels said God heard his prayer and granted his request.

"When they started doing the surgery, the doctor said, 'now I know I saw that he needed a stent. Then he said, I don't see that anymore.'"

God had healed it, and I was so happy...

"After the doctor didn't find anything, the doctor told me that I didn't need the surgery," Daniels said. "He said, Mr. Daniels, your arteries are good. I immediately started thanking the Lord. I actually thanked the Lord before I went in because I knew he would heal me. I've seen God work, and I've seen Him move in the lives of His people. I thank Him for that. I thank Him for healing me. When you have faith and trust in the Lord, regardless of what the doctor says or what it looks like, I am a living witness that by totally trusting God, He can remove the obstacle you're about to encounter. That's what He did for me, and if you trust Him and put your faith in Him, He will do it for you too."

GOD HEALED ME OF A MEDICAL CONDITION THAT HAS NO CURE

DELCENIA DANIELS
Holly Springs, Mississippi

Walking around and being able to visit with family and friends has always been something that brought joy to Delcenia Daniels, but when she was diagnosed with neuropathy in her legs in 2004, putting her faith and trust in God for healing and deliverance was the only thing she could do.

"The doctors told me that there's no cure for neuropathy," Daniels recalled. According to The Mayo Clinic, neuropathy is the gradual onset of numbness, prickling or tingling in a person's feet or hands, which can spread upward into their legs and arms with sharp, jabbing, throbbing, freezing or burning pain, or extreme sensitivity to touch. More than 20 million people in the United States have some form of neuropathy.

"I had gotten to the place to where I couldn't walk," Daniels said. "I'm a diabetic, and I had reached a point in my life to where my legs hurt so bad that when I walked, my legs would come out from under me. I would have to ask people when I went some place to put my legs in the car for me."

Daniels stressed that not being able to walk on her own as she had done her entire life is something that weighed on her. Being a Christian woman of faith, she said, placing her faith in Jesus Christ is what changed everything for her.

I started praying that God would heal my legs so that I would be able to walk...

"I was sitting in church one Sunday, and I don't know what happened, but it was like fire shut up in my bones, and I knew how Jeremiah felt (Jeremiah 20:9)," Daniels described. "All of a sudden, I was able to walk all over the church without my stick, without hopping, without my crutch, without anything."

Daniels stressed that her faith in God resulted in being delivered from a condition in which man (doctors) said there was no cure for.

"I was able to put my medication down," said Daniels, who has not had to take any medication related to neuropathy in more than 12 years. "God healed my neuropathy, although they say there's no cure. It was all a result of having faith in Him. If He healed me through faith, then He can heal someone else too. Just put your faith and trust in Him."

CHAPTER 23
PURPOSE

BY TRUSTING GOD'S GUIDANCE, I DISCOVERED MY PURPOSE

BRANDI JO PAYNE
Pascagoula, Mississippi

As a child growing up in a Christian home, Brandi Jo Payne was taught that having faith meant trusting God even though you can't see what God is doing in your life, but it wasn't until she graduated from college and looking to start her career that what she had been taught all of her life became a reality.

"For two whole years I was applying for jobs, and I only received one callback," said Payne, who graduated from the University of Southern Mississippi with a bachelor of arts in criminal justice. "I had a plan for my life, and in my own mind, I knew what I wanted to do. However, the plans I had for myself just wasn't working out the way I thought they would."

It was a frustrating time, but I decided to let go and let God...

Payne said she found herself in the same position that many college students find themselves in: with a college degree, with student loans, and unable to find a job in their field of study.

"But once I allowed God to do what He wanted to do in my life, that's when I found my true purpose in life," Payne said, before adding, "an opportunity came up to where I was able to work in a school in New Orleans. I discovered that I had a natural gift for working with and teaching children."

Payne said that she also realized that although she had gone to college and received a degree in criminal justice and forensic science when she looked back over her life, she realized that God had been preparing her for teaching her entire life.

"Growing up, I've always had to babysit for my aunts, cousins, other family members and friends, and I never saw this gift

I have, but God did," Payne said. "Now, I know my true passion and my reason for being here. My testimony is that having faith in God and trusting Him even when you can't see what He is up to is the best thing anyone can do. You never know, He may just be trying to bring out a hidden talent or gift that you don't know you have. I went out on faith to trust Him, and once I did that, He stepped in."

Today Payne works as a special education instructor in Pascagoula, Mississippi.

AFTER I HAD THE FAITH TO GO ON FAITH, MY FIRST BOOK WAS PUBLISHED

KEVIN MITCHELL
Kansas City, Kansas

After leaving corporate America in 2004, Kevin Mitchell spent time consulting God on what was next for his life. Little did he know that God would reveal a hidden gift that he never knew he had. However, it required a demonstration of his faith to give birth to his newly found gift designed to be shared with the world.

"God has shown me that I have this gift of writing sports books," Mitchell said. "This is something that I didn't realize I had, and I've had no training in journalism in terms of education. I've taken no creative writing class, but this gift that He has given me to write has been a faith walk. Since 2004 when I left corporate America, I've been on a faith walk where I've been totally dependent upon God."

On March 5, 2015, Mitchell's first book, Last Train to Cooperstown, was released to the world...

"That was a blessing," said Mitchell.

Last Train to Cooperstown uncovers and brings to light, the deep, unshakable, and everlasting roots African Americans have in America's great game of baseball.

"I've written articles, I have a blog, and it just seems as though the things that I write are not inspirational or new revelation on scripture or anything like that, but I still believe that everything that I write, it has come from God," Mitchell said.

Mitchell went on to note that his story of faith is actually him having the faith to go on faith.

"I don't know where it's going to end, or where it's going to lead to, or how successful I'm going to be," Mitchell said.

I'm just trusting in Him each day as I go, but I know that this is the destiny that He has for me...

Mitchell stressed that he knows that what God is looking for from him is a display of faith, and not just simply talk or for him to "say" he has faith.

"He is looking for a demonstration of my faith, and that is for me to just keep going forward, and no matter how uncertain things may be, no matter how much adversity I may run into, but He just wants me to demonstrate the faith that I claim I have in Him," said Mitchell.

Mitchell's blog, The Baseball Scroll, is at *klmitchell.com*.

"LIKE SAUL'S NAME WAS CHANGED TO PAUL, THROUGH FAITH, I ACCEPTED CHRIST & HAD A TRUE CONVERSION EXPERIENCE

PASTOR LEROY JAMES
Memphis, Tennessee

Leroy James grew up in a family of preachers and believers of Christianity, but to him, it was all nonsense, that is until he says God called him to serve in His ministry.

He says just as Saul in Acts 9:1-19 was converted to Paul on Damascus Road, he says God did the same thing to him during the first week of July 1980, and that his faith in Christ is a testimony to others who have fought the call to ministry, or are currently fighting the call into God's ministry.

"I felt the anointing of God moving on me, but I didn't understand what it was," James stressed. "I used to criticize Christians. I criticized people in the church. I talked about them. I even had brothers and grandfathers, uncles, cousins who were preaching. I just felt like all of that was not necessary. But one day I was sitting in the house watching TV before my 3-11 p.m. work shift, and I heard a preacher on TV say, "You can run, but you can't hide. That bothered me. I got my lunch and went on to work. My mind kept going back to 'you can run, but you can't hide.' That stayed on my mind all night long. I couldn't even eat because that was bothering me so bad. All I could hear is, 'you can run, but you can't hide.'"

A week or two after that, the power of God really started moving...I was scared, and I didn't know what to do...

"I wasn't an alcoholic or drug addict, but I wanted that 'you can run, but you can't hide' to go away. I got in my car because I wanted to get the voice of 'you can run, but you can't hide' out of me. I stopped at a liquor store. I had never drunk liquor in my life, but I felt like if I could drink some liquor, the 'you can run, but you can't hide' wouldn't bother me anymore. So I started sipping the liquor, and my mind told me to go across the bridge in West Memphis, Arkansas. I started driving, and the liquor started talking to me, telling me that I needed to drive a little faster, so the police can catch you and put you in jail."

I intentionally drove fast enough in order to get arrested...

"Ordinarily, you would get arrested driving this particular road in Arkansas at a high rate of speed, but I didn't get arrested," James recalled. "I started praying and asking God, what is it, but He didn't respond right away. But that Sunday (the first week in July 1980), I went to church, and God said, 'Get up.' I didn't know what He meant, but it led me to the altar, that's where I got on my knees. I said, 'God, what is it that you want?' He did not respond. That Monday after Sunday's church service, that's when God really started moving on me."

His spirit started moving and touching me; the whole week from Monday through Friday, all I did was shed tears, pleading with God to please tell me what is it that you want me to do...

"At 1:01 in the morning that Saturday, I felt the power of God moving over me," James stressed. "It started at my legs. It felt like somebody kept pouring warm water on me. It went from my leg, all the way up my thigh, all the way up my chest, all the way on my head. When I opened my eyes, I could feel just a glance of light in my bed. There were no lights on in the room, no lights on in the house, but I could see this light. I saw God moving upon me by a shining light."

That's when I stood up in the bed, I started shouting, I started praising God, and that's when I accepted God...

"I said, Lord, hear am I, take me, Lord, take me, Lord, please take me," James recalled. "And ever since then, I've been pleading for God to use me. For 36 years, God has been using me."

James, who has been the Pastor of Hopewell M.B. Church in Holly Springs, Mississippi for more than 22 years, said his conversion experience is an encouragement to the church and to those who are afraid to accept Christ. He says accepting Christ, living out his call to preach the Gospel, and living as a Christian should, is not easy. He noted that hard times and disappointments are all part of the process after accepting Christ as Lord and Savior.

"I accepted Christ and the call to preach, but there have been many times where I've left the church in which I pastor and said to myself that I wasn't coming back, but every Sunday morning, for the past 22 years, God leads me back to Hopewell M.B. Church, because there are people who still need to be saved."

WITH GOD, I OVERCAME FINANCIAL LOSS & WALKED INTO MY PURPOSE

ROBERT BANKS, JR

New Orleans, Louisia

Ask Robert Banks Jr. how he is doing on any given day, and he'll quickly reply with a glowing smile and whispering sweet voice, "God is good."

Had you asked him that very same question some 25 years ago, his answer might have been the complete opposite. But most people would never know it looking at him from the outside today.

His nearly six-foot tall, solid frame; strong yet gentle handshake gives off a sense of strength. With a slow pace, he can be seen at his home church on Sunday's graciously walking around greeting and encouraging worshipers as if he has no worry in the world. But when he opens up and pulls back the curtain of his life, this calm-spirited man's story gives hope to those who may feel like giving up.

Loss and Restoration

Banks had it all—At least he thought he did. He was a young man full of life. He owned his own business, making more money than he could have ever imagined. He was married. He had kids. He simply had it going on. Whatever he wanted to eat, he ate it. Wherever he and his family wanted to travel, he had enough money in the bank to make it happen.

In fact, in the 1970s, the American Dream, according to Banks, was to live in a suburban home with a white picket fence, a wife, and kids. But for Banks, this wasn't just a dream. It was his reality—a life of styling, profiling, and living it up as the young folk today would say. Life was good!

But like a hurricane, Banks' life suddenly spun out of control. He found himself in the eye of a storm that destroyed what seemed like everything in sight, leaving him with nothing.

"It was one of the hardest times in my life," he said.

Banks, in 1989, was the owner of a lucrative excavating business in Jefferson Parish, located in the New Orleans-Metairie, Louisiana metropolitan area, where he utilized heavy equipment (tractors, bulldozers) to earn more than $2,000 in an hour. That's good money in any economy. It was good money in Banks' mind too, that is until personal trials and tribulations hit.

I lost everything, my wife left me, my children left me, even the dog left me....

"I started idolizing the heavy equipment and depending on money rather than on God," Banks stressed. "I idolized the equipment so much that just like some people today have gold crosses on their neck, I had a gold-plated dump truck around my neck. I was putting all of this before God."

Like uncontained rain bands forming swiftly on the outside of a Category 5 hurricane, Banks' life became unglued with unsuspecting winds, chaos, and destruction showing up on every turn. But instead of seeking God, Banks, just as he had done so successfully in the past, tried to "fix" his way out of the storm by the only way he knew how: with money.

But that didn't work.

"Business had come to a complete stop," Banks recalled. "No contracts were coming in and the banks in which I financed everything with just started seizing stuff, right in front of me, right in front of people who knew me for years, right in front of people who knew how much of a successful business person I was."

He was embarrassed, to say the least. Banks, who had gained so much in terms of wealth, happiness, and family, was now drowning deep in a season of loss.

"The Mercedes I drove as a personal vehicle was taken from me by the banks," he said. "I had to lay off staff, and just when I didn't think things could get any worse, the IRS came into my office and conducted an open-house audit. I ended up owing over $26,000."

But it didn't end there. Local vendors started calling Banks about approximately 30 bad checks that had been written. The checks, Banks says, were written by a former employee, but ultimately he was responsible for the bad checks. In order to resolve the bad checks, Banks had to go through the pain, humiliation, and emotional hurt of having his personal finances on public display in and out of the courts for everyone to see.

"I had problem after problem," he said. "It seemed like once I got one problem fixed, another problem came."

I had never ever thought about ending my life, but one morning I found myself sitting at the edge of my bed with a .357 gun in my hand…

There sitting alone in his room with tears streaming down his face, with no sense of hope, feeling defeated, Banks thought about all the things he had lost, all the time, blood, sweat, and tears he put into building his business. All of it, now gone. He sat there, in a state of depression, and lack, personally and financially. With his head down, he stared at the .357 gun he held in his hand. Visualizing and remembering the good life he once had, compared to the emptiness he felt at that very moment, his hands squeezed the gun tighter and tighter.

Banks, with his burdens cast on his shoulders, his heart beating faster and faster, thumping powerfully, as though his heart was jumping out of his shirt. His hand started to rise upward. He was finally ready to do it!

But then the phone rang. "I jumped," he said.

It was a Divine phone call.

"I'll never forget," Banks said. "It was my play sister. I don't have any biological sisters, so I call her my play sister. As we spoke, she knew that something wasn't right with me. She had no idea what I had been going through, but her discerning spirit led her to pray for me right then and there. She prayed for me like no one had ever openly prayed for me. When we finished praying, I saw the gun in my hand. I asked myself the question, "What is this gun doing in my hand? What am I doing with this? I automatically put it back on the nightstand. And from that day forward, my life made a 360-degree turn for the Lord."

Banks says his testimony is that God allowed Satan to bring him down to such a point in his life to where his faith had to be re-routed back to Jesus Christ.

"The Lord allowed me to get to the point to where I solely depended on Him," he said.

My life took a turn from the worst to the best in Jesus Christ...

"Sometimes He has to clean the rough edges off of us, and that's what He did in my life in order for me to learn to have faith," he said. "God has a way of drawing you back to Him. I had to fulfill my purpose of preaching the Gospel. I was called to preach the Word of God at the age of 12, and after this faith-testing time in my life, I was able to walk into my calling as a minister and work in prison ministry preaching all over the world."

Banks went on to note that the lesson he learned while going through his personal storm and testing of his faith, is that by living his life trusting only in God, everything that he lost, returned—His business thrived again. Today, he is married, and he has a close relationship with his children.

"Often times when I would put in bids for contracts, people would tell me that they didn't understand why they were giving the contract to me because my bid was higher than others," Banks said, before adding, "Although they didn't understand it, I did. It was God rewarding me for my faith in Him."